Encountering the
Power of God

Encountering the Power of God

**The Reality of Life Deserves Spiritual
Attention to Mandate Its Rightful Destiny**

REV. STEPHEN HAMILTON

authorHOUSE®

AuthorHouse™ UK
1663 Liberty Drive
Bloomington, IN 47403 USA
www.authorhouse.co.uk
Phone: 0800.197.4150

Cover designed by Vertruaen Active Link
Typeset and edited by: Christopher Nuamah

Published by AuthorHouse 07/29/2015

ISBN: 978-1-5049-4253-9 (sc)
ISBN: 978-1-5049-4249-2 (e)

Print information available on the last page.

Contents

Contents

This divinely directed written book is first dedicated to the Lord and Saviour Jesus Christ, who through his wisdom made the writing of this book a success.

To my wife, Beatrice Hamilton; may God bless you for your great support in both prayer and logistics for all these years behind me in this ministry. Also to all my leaders in the ministry of Victory Outreach International.

To Rev. Frank Osei, the founder of Victory Charismatic Chapel; your assistance to my establishment will never sink in my heart. God bless you.

To the editor, Christopher Nuamah, in Victory Outreach International; thank you for the great work, making this book well appraised and edited for reading.

Thanks to Assistant Pastor Fofovi Calise Amendon. God bless you for your anticipated cooperation. Also thanks to all the members of Victory Outreach International; God bless you all.

Preface

Encountering the Power of God is a must-read book for everyone who cares and regards success in life, irrespective of logistics and one's academic and spiritual background. This book will convince and educate you on how the power of God can change your story, because in the spiritual battle it is only God who can intervene to reverse the undesirable trends of your destiny. The book is highly recommended for victims of spiritual battle.

—Rev. Stephen Hamilton (Papa)

I have been reading many books on God's interventions and its effect, and I have come to realize that we must grow in spirit. If we don't grow, we cannot have fellowship with God, for God is a spirit, and they who worship him must worship him in spirit and in truth.

—Beatrice Hamilton (Mama)

In our generation, we are bearing the fruits of our forefathers and sowing a new seed for the future of our children. In order to be able to understand your fruited way of life, you must determine the definition of your religious zeal of worship. Historically the fruit of life can germinate to cause a lot of hazards to people in the family, depending on the covenant relationship implemented to rule the family. This is an historic covenant, and to deal or fight it out defines the new seed you sow as a result of good future for your children. Therefore your responsibility to fight it is a mantel of heavy infantry which cannot be done by the flesh but by the power from the supernatural.

Life's success deserves the attention given to it through the process of breakthrough; this perception works in so many ways that afflict prescribed ways and means that are substituted to evil, and it then it gives its trademark of misery, which is the simple way that Satan uses to have us in his hand.

I am much convinced that God has given me the intellectual writing capability to spread his word across the world and to make his ways known to the multitude, in order to make man change from evil encounters through a divine process and encounter the power of God.

Introduction

Nature is the origin of everything, and it refines those who seek the route because it is the work you pursue in order to know much about your history. Your history tells you where you are coming from, and through that you will come across the domain of prosperity or curse that reincarnated in your family. This process will draw your attention to eventual occurrences in your life, and then you begin to think very widely, but the only thing your mindset can preview is the surface of imagination on what might be the cause. Even so, you might get it all wrong because this is about spiritual covenant and encountering power; it is beyond your ability to predict the source and the outcome regardless of your intellectual rigor and the legitimate assistance of your trusted repository.

Our forefathers had their routes of encounters, and their power of inheritance has transmitted it to our current lives. Many have died without being responsible for the cause; many are also enjoying historic encounters with their forefathers. This tells you that encountering a power is a very serious experience that we automatically come across in our lives depending on where we are coming from, and it defines our routes.

Furthermore, civilization has brought out modern living today, but you still bear the fruit of your forefathers. It is likely that your history still has something to do with your current life. The ignorance of mankind in this area has plugged a lot of people into misery. Satan uses ignorance to escape the mind and the historical covenant of your forefathers, having an effect on your life currently. I am not surprised at the level of acceleration in ignorance in the world today, and of the historic ignorance across national boundaries, because reality of life is the enemy to the belief of historical ignorance. Will this problem continue to plague mankind?

The world is now out of control, and who is responsible? Is it our forefathers' atrocities or our current sins? You might think your route has nothing to do with the spiritual covenant because you have survived in life, but I want you to understand that because you bear the fruit of Adam and Eve, you cannot change your history. Satan, the devil who couldn't stand fast in the truth of the Kingdom of God, brought sin into the world (John 8: 44); he instigated and succeeded in the Garden of Eden (Gen. 3: 1–5). Mankind followed him and ignored the good ways of the creator.

The ignorance here symbolizes the fictitious redemption of mankind, which is slavery. The deceit was the context of the activism that took place between man and God, and its harvest is what we experience today. Mankind's ignorance has already taken place in ages, and we are bearing the implications today. I want you to understand that you take responsibility for what you say and your actions, and therefore the future of your children is reliant on your covenant today. Sow a seed that will bear good fruits for the benefit of your children and your entire generation. I bring to your doorstep the cause of your problems, as well as its solution in a different dimension, to establish everlasting progression and a total force that can defeat the kingdom of Satan: encountering the power of God. This supernatural control deals with the major attacks of Satan.

There are so many ways we create problems for ourselves. In our normal lives, we consider so many things as problems, but they are not because we lack the logical experience. You are entitled to logical thinking as a required tool for solving your minor problems. Sometimes you lack research before a transaction takes place, but think about normal, minor situations that demand the rules of common sense in order to deal with them. They are not more difficult than problems we inherit from our forefathers or our generation through covenants. By encountering the power of God, the yoke will be broken, the iron gate will open, and the chains will be released from your hands. These devilish weapons of family covenants killing us today describe how strong it indulges in the fount of the covenant, and our problems today prove how powerful the source of the curse in our lives is, and how difficult it is to have our breakthroughs. However, by encountering the power of God, all the bondages will come to an end.

> Lift up the heads, O you gates! And be lifted up, you everlasting doors! And the king of glory shall come in Who is the king of glory? The lord strong and mighty, the lord mighty in battle.

> Lift up your heads O you gates! Lift up your everlasting doors! And the kings of glory shall come in Who is the king of glory? The lord of hosts, He is the king of glory. (Ps. 24: 7–10)

Chapter 1

A Vibrant Key Factor Before, During, and after the Encounter of God

A covenant is the submission of the heart, mind, and soul to promise with affirmed restriction and to engage in an agreement with God. It takes a required process that has both retribution and impartation significance, depending on your attention and value given to it before, during, and after the encounter. This process invokes spiritual power to approve and assign function. A spiritual covenant with God is the sacrifice you pronounce and react upon, and it deserves the attention of obedience and submission; through that you have adjusted a closed door to encounter the power of God.

Historically a power encounter is sealed by a covenant, and before you can make a sensitive approach for a breakthrough, you need to know the secret of your covenant. You may think, "So how can I know the secret of my family covenant transgressing upon me?" The only logical answer that comes to your repository is to ask your parents or a relative, but I want to prove to you that what your mother might tell you might be different from what your uncle or relative will tell you, because history always has three sides of the story to be told: what you hear, who narrates it, and the truth that stands on its own. The only man to tell you the true secret is the Most High God, and he is the obscurity of nature and knows all that happens both in darkness and light. If you believe God created heaven and earth, made man as in his own image, and placed him in the garden of Eden, and that man was tempted by Satan, then God gave man the mandate of how woman will suffer before giving birth, and man will work for the fruits of his labour. This powerful declaration from God has had an effect to this day.

This fact clearly tells you the reality about historic covenants having an effect on our current lives. The only intervention to reverse undesirable trends of turbulence from our forefathers is the power of God. Implementations governing the sector of your belief are recommended by researchers and historians, and that might seems to be the resolved scheme to rely upon. I want to tell you today that it will be the greatest mistake ever you will make, if your attention has nothing to do with God's power of intervention but is on fictitious discovery of the force of gravity and other scientific things. Inheriting names, titles, properties, and ceremonies has a covenant significance in your history and affects your current life.

In addition, this life portage connects you to your history. Your interest or forbiddance doesn't matter when it comes to lineage; this is a leverage identity of where you come from, and you undertake the responsibility of automatically complying with rules of the family. This is not about choice but a zeal of spiritual force compliance, of which you might not even be aware. Some family ceremonies have historic associations with spirits in the darkness that fight against good marriage, because they have a marriage covenant with women in the family. Others have titles of spirit that deal with evil power, and so they suffer from premature deaths; though you can see them succeeding in life, they die early and unexpectedly.

Names are common ones we come across, and we sometimes speak against them due to our understanding of the meaning of the name. You can choose not to use the name anymore, but that does not mean you are free from your problems, because it is already tied into the spiritual world. Something must be done before you can overthrow the ruler of your name. Jacob experience a change of name, and God decided to change it. Name meaning is very important, and your name reveals a lot about your personality and your past and future. The problems you are facing continuously might be because of your name. You have already taken the assignment of your name the moment the name is given to you by who gave birth to you. You take the responsibilities of the reasons, and it affects you. Name is a covenanted seal to your future and is a power that dominates the destiny. Moses's name means "drawn out of water" – it's no wonder that water played a prominent role in his calling: He changed water to blood, he brought water out of rock, and he crossed the Red Sea with the Israelites.

> No longer shall your name be called Abram but your name shall be Abraham, for you have made you a father of many nations. I will make you exceedingly

> fruitful; and I will make nation of you and kings shall come from you. And I will establish my covenant between me and you and your descendants after you in their generation for an everlasting covenant," to be God to you and your descendant after you. Also, I give you your descendant after you the land in which you are strangers and all the land of Canaan, as an everlasting possession and I will be their God. (Gen. 17;5–8)

God changed Abram to Abraham, changing the meaning from "exalted father" to "Father of many nations". Whatever may be the name that has been working against you, after reading this book and applying what it recalls, you can encounter the power of God, your name will be changed from bad to good, and your victory will be apparent for your enemies to bear witness.

Jabez started out on a bad note the day he was born: he was named "child of sorrow". One day he got fed up with being called sorrow, and he cried to God, saying, "My mother called me Sorrow, and everybody who knows my name identifies me as a sorrow. I want you to change my name, and I want you to bless me. I want you to lay your hand upon my life, and I don't want to have anything to do with sorrow." If your parents had an encounter with evil, it is likely to have effect on their children, and it takes the grace of God for even one of the children to survive. The only way is to encounter the power of God that will set you free. Just one person amongst the siblings or in the family can encounter the power of God, and the rest can be set free.

God is so wonderful and has so many ways of setting us free. Many people are running away from the truth and want to be free, but it's only the truth that can set them free because their truth is their covenant. The destination of their hideout might be the camp of their problems. Sometimes we implement certain non-existing policies in order to solve our problems, just by the influence of friends' intellect and of books written by scholars.

A member of my ministry shared with me his past when he was in the world. He was ruled and controlled by evil spirit, and I felt like crying. I allowed myself to do so – fighting back tears was futile, and I felt relief after. I know that not every person grieves in the same way. because suppressing your emotions might not be your way, but your outward expression does not display tears at times. After he spoke, God said through me to him that problems have a duration to be dealt with before they fester, and the more they fester, the more they turn into (public) ugly episodes. This is similar to repentance: the duration of repentance is known by no man, but one day there will be no chance to repent, all will be over, and you will meet judgement.

Many are frustrated by their life problems, but they have forgotten to seek the required solution to the problems. This is where the devil will consume you and convince you to commit suicide. Suicide is connected to the mindset after frustration has taken place. Many have committed suicide as a result of an uncontrollable situation. Today as you read this book, keep it in your mental faculty. Whenever disappointment comes your way, see it as an experience to move ahead in life.

Where are you going, and what do you want? You are responsible for your own problems. There are people who call themselves intellectuals, but they passionately hate the

Bible because they view it as the book of the oppressor. These people do so in ignorance, neglecting the fact that the real author of the Bible is not the humans but the spirit of God. It comes as a shock to them to discover that the Bible contains messages of the truth, reality, and power that rule the world. The rules of the world created by God are static in nature – no one can change them. Many will continue to doubt, and they will continue to be in misery until they change their ways to Christ and encounter the power of God.

You have known the truth, but you still seem to be taken away by the world. You are a happy person in the daytime, roaming with aimless friends, but you cry at night in bed. Why can't you give your life to Christ, where you will be free forever? Today as you read this book, I command the spirit of God to encounter your soul. Encountering the power of God is a divine mandate that grants you eternal life, and all your problems and difficulties will be addressed by God himself. It is very important to identify the way, the truth, and the life because no one will go to the Father except through Jesus Christ. Therefore the way is your repentance, the truth is the word, and the life is the kingdom of heaven. It is very important to learn the truth about the condition of the encounter; God is not a respecter of person, and irrespective of your background and the level of your intellect, you qualify to experience the power of God. Don't get confused: the condition here simply means the way you choose to solve your problems.

In addition, in order to be able to identify the required keys to solve your problems, you must define who you are and how useful you are to you family, friends, and the nation. What are your ways of solving your problems? It is then necessary to read books, which serve as guides to solve your problems and move you to a different level in life so that you can achieve your goals beyond your expectations. You sometimes consider your life to be of no use to the environment and the people around you, and it takes the encounter of God to change your story. Two childhood friends grew up together, but life became very difficult for them. One decided to travel as the solution to his problem because he considered the environment as the cause to his problems; the other decided to inquire about his route because he considered a spiritual attack as the cause of an historic, unseen covenant. Both of them proceeded, and the one with spiritual ignorance found himself in desperation and died in three years' time. The one who had the thought of a spiritual unseen covenant as the cause baited the hook and found out that yes, it bites, and that the only way was to accept Jesus Christ as his personal saviour. In line with his process, he encountered the power of God and had a breakthrough. That is the innocent heart compensated by the grace.

God knows your heart regardless of all accusations reflecting on your profile. He will change your story only if you accept the reality of life and believe that God can intervene. Run to him for divine breakthrough, which I am introducing to you now as the divine encounter. A medical doctor who never attended church in his life conducted research about divine encounter. Throughout all his research, he came across a simple definition related to his field of profession: "A medical encounter form is a document that is used to collect all the relevant information of a patient whenever he/ she visits a health facility. This form is used by the medical providers to minimize inconsistencies and validate entries."

He sat back in his chair and connected to creation. He then realized he was making a mistake of lacking knowledge about spiritual reality and the power of encounter. The point here is that regardless of your intelligence, God speaks in parables, and it takes one who believes to have the heart of understanding.

> But others fell on good grounds, sprang up, and yielded a crop hundred folds. When he said these things he cried, "he who has ears to hear, let them hear!" Then the disciples asked him, saying, "what does this parable mean?" and he said, to you it has been given to know the mysteries of the kingdom of God but the rest it is given in parables, that seeing they may not see, and hearing they may not understand. Now the parable is this: The seed is the word of God. (Luke 8: 8–11)

The word is a parable to those who don't know Christ, and they will never understand. The first day God revealed this verse to me, I realized that the strength of Satan is deceiving many by pulling them into scriptural litigation. I want to prove to you that our prosperity in marriage, businesses, finance, and ministry depends on the encounter we experience – there cannot be a success without a sacrifice. Covenant plays a vital role as a valued sacrifice endorsement to experience the encounter for your breakthrough of expectations.

Covenant stands for power when encountering avails; it takes place before experiencing the encountering, though encountering the power of God takes place unexpectedly at a particular point in time. But before that, a process has taken place, whether we are aware or unaware. It can be a practical form, it can be a given direction (like worship) or it can even be a strong and powerful dialogue from our tongue. That is why we need to be careful about the words that come out of our mouths.

This book will enlighten you regarding the reality of spiritually encountering the power of God, as well as the steps to guide and educate you on how the encountering connects you to the Holy Spirit. The Holy Spirit plays a vital role in your encounter: he complies with your faith, and through that you will make a sensitive approach to the everlasting, protected miracle so that your life can be transformed.

A great kingdom was facing a problem whereby kids were vanishing from various locations. The king of the village did his best to find out where these children were disappearing to, but there was no rectification and no solution. The king employed special investigation teams from various places, but they couldn't find the children, and there was no trace in any of the investigated reports. The king vowed to divide all he had into two equal parts, and he would give one-half to anybody who will be able to find these children. For many years this kingdom kept bleeding. One day, a convict broke out of jail. On his way through a forest, he came across where these innocent children had been disappearing to, and he managed to prove what his eyes were witnessing. He later reported to the king and he was honoured with the reward.

Life is not always how we think it should be, but when God puts you there, no matter where you are coming from, you will be the head and not the tail. Never think you can't survive, because many are accusing you and pointing fingers at you. This convict encountered the power of God, and he won the battle. May you come across your prosperity after reading this book, in the name of Jesus. It is only God who can change your story depending on your covenant with him; he can convert an ordinary event into a significant one. Whenever a man has an encounter with God, his story changes from bad to good. Moses was running away from his alleged murdered culprit, but he came through the encounter, and God choose him to undertake a highly responsible assignment.

No matter the sin you have committed, God still loves you. Run to him, confess your sins, and repent to be born again. Believe in your heart that you have been forgiven and that God is ready to forgive you. There is a need for you to understand the love of God. God is not a respecter of men, and he looks into your heart and lifts you up. Seeking an evil encounter as the solution to your problem worsens the problem, and it will destroy you. The power of God is the only way to deal with every historic covenant affecting your life. Your problems and obstacles cannot kill you, if you encounter the power of God. You will be surprised how simple it is when you begin to understand that a covenant with God is the key factor in order to experience the power of God. God has the power, and having an encounter with him does not require qualification or diplomacy – it simply needs your fulfilment of the covenant with him. This tells you that your problems are solved, as you read this book in the name of Jesus.

Chapter 2

What Is Encountering?

Encountering is a practical process of portraying results of an experience. It happens in the form of positive or negative, trending to impartation or diminishment. Encountering the power of God has a structure of transformation depending on the source and the destination. For you to encounter an evil spirit or the power of God, it requires you to undertake principles of vision in order to carry out an apprehended mission. There are various principles of life that accelerate an encounter, but notice that whether experiencing power encountered by evil or by God, it rules your life and controls it to its direction because it has put itself together and needs to function. This means that if you encounter the power of evil, your life will be controlled by evil, and its effect will be destruction and distortion; it will plug you into misery, and you will be a slave for evil.

> When an unclean spirit goes out of a man, he goes through a dry place seeking rest; and finding none,

he says, I will return to my house from which I came.
(Luke 11: 24)

Experiencing an evil encounter automatically afflicts all your opportunities in life because it is covered by darkness, and there is no way that peace will be your portion. You cannot find peace and redemption in darkness; in the same way, darkness has no power over light because where there is light, you cannot see darkness. Encountering operates in the spiritual realm before you experience it, and God is faithful because salvation took place for the redemption of mankind through his only begotten son, Jesus Christ, who serves as a light for sinners to run to. Therefore you have already encountered the power of forgiveness, you are no more in the hands of the devil, and you don't fall within darkness. You simply have to believe that the son of God came to manifest and render salvation. The Holy Spirit came upon the disciples to activate the redemptive right for salvation. You have to choose who rules your life, darkness or light. Don't choose one because of its definition or description, because each has a principle guiding its effect. The way you live your life will determine where you are and who controls it. You were carried in a womb for nine months before you were conceived, and that is a divine purpose delivery; your appearance on earth was not an accident or mistake. I entreat you to value your life. Sometimes I wonder why one jeopardises his life of redemption for the sake of wealth. Valuation of wealth more than life is a sin against creation, and it is a curse.

Encountering doesn't take place without you setting up a target for yourself, which is a target for prosperity, breakthrough, or victory. It is the basis that gives you the divine mandate of encountering the power. These relevant keys describe your motivational access of encountering the power of God.

1. Vision
2. Mission
3. Spiritual preservation
4. Sacrifice
5. Faith
6. Obedience

These are the elements that determine your steps of encountering the power of God. A lazy man who never anticipates spiritual cooperation simply relaxes and imagines how to get there. Imagination is the foresight that strengthens your mandate, but without the attributes of the required mission, you can never make it.

From Genesis to Revelation, no man has been rewarded according to his laziness. Therefore I recommend the zeal of a spiritual guide to assist you in making a step towards your encounter with God's power.

Vision

The faculty of success in life is the target you set for yourself and your work towards it. This gives you the mandate of researching for the means and ways to get there. Without the route of the tree, you cannot harvest the fruit, so the seed needs to be planted and preserved for future harvest, and all the necessary fertilization needed will be provided by a wise and determined gardener. Your vision will determine your life plan, and it will process your duties in that line of what you encounter the power of God, but only if you consider him as the ultimate guide to the destination of your vision. Though you will come across obstacles in life, you have your map, and the encountering will get you there unexpectedly. I want you to understand that in every successful destination there is an obstacle, and the only key to break that obstacle is staying in focus with faith. This is a unique, static leverage of success. Do make note of it because a lot of temptation will come your way; this is a signal of the odds surrounding your victory, so keep your head up and call unto his name the Jehovah.

God matters when it comes to your vision, and though he always wants the best for you, sometimes your vision might not be the will and wish of God. People get confused here, but it is very simple. If you set up a good vision for yourself and work towards it, God shapes it beyond your expectations. You wanted this, but God gave you that, and it will surely be better than what you originally wanted. I encourage you to have trust in God if you have chosen him to be your vision plot point. If you have set up that point of vision, then I can assure you that you will encounter the power of God, and your transformation in life will be beyond your prediction.

Visions are not to predict the mind of people around you, or to persuade others to like you. Sometimes you lie to impress people around you. If your friend has a similar vision and has been able to attain to it, you ask yourself, "How did he do it? What was his source of power? And how will he end it?" It is good to be motivated by accomplishments of others, but I advise you not to jump into the scale of the moment and call it a vision. It is the worst captivity in which we indulge. You need to be sincere and faithful to yourself; understand the outcome of vision projection.

Although vision is power and has to be secret, conducting research about your vision is not a form of broadcasting what you want to do. Don't fall victim to creating a platform for your enemies to seek revenge for their defeat. You need to be careful about those with whom you share your vision and plan, because they might be your dream killers. In short, your vision must be your secret, so have the foresight to have your encounter with the power of God. Adequate spiritual wisdom needs to be applied during the process of your encounter with God.

Mission

The mandate of your vision is the determination of your mission, and the vision can never have a platform without configuring the mission. This indicates your two-vessel foresight in life. Mission is therefore considered to be one of the great accesses to encountering the power of God because it makes you self-equip, which gives you the determination to come closer to God if you realise who has power to the throne.

How do you carry your assignment?

Do you know that spiritually you are assigned to a target, and without the encounter, you will deviate? Under what circumstances do you figure your opportunities in life without heaping the vow to encounter the power of God? If you are determined to succeed in life, the question is how do you get there without undertaking a vibrant mission of a great vision? These questions define a great misery in your life if you fall victim to its culprit, but at the same time they can define a great, successful person if you fall under the norms of living your life.

Faith

> And what shall I say? for the time would fail me to tell of Gideon and Barak and Samson and Jephthah, also of David and Samuel and the prophets: who through faith subdued kingdoms, work righteousness, obtained promises, stopped the mouth of lions, quenched the violence of fire, escaped the edge of the sword, out of weakness were made strong, became valiant in battle, turned to flight the armies of the aliens. (Heb. 11: 32–34)

Faith plays a vital role in your encountering, because this is a spiritual journey that connects you to your vision and mission. Your vision determines your mission, and so faith becomes the integral focal point of your mission statement undersigned by your spiritual legitimacy for a battle. It takes faith for mankind to believe in what you have never seen, and it takes faith for you to believe in the reality of nature. Jesus said, "Let not your heart be troubled. You believe in God, believe also in me. Is not my authority but the father who dwell in me does the work. Believe in me that I am the father and the father in me or else believes me for the sake of the works themselves? I do not speak by my own" (John 14: 1–10) I will prove to you that if you believe in God, then you are automatically closer to the encounter.

The one whom he sent laid emphasis on your helper when he was going to heaven. He said, "I will not leave you as orphans but give you another helper and he will abide with you forever, he is the spirit of the truth whom the world cannot receive because it neither sees him nor knows him" (John 14: 16–17). If you have a sense of doubting the creator because you don't see him, then you are under a curse. The same applies to the helper who is the Holy Spirit and who lives with us on the earth forever. The Holy Spirit was sent to us by the father in the name of his son, Jesus Christ. He will teach you all things, including how to encounter the power of God, because God is greater than the son, but it takes faith for you to acquire the divine guidance of the Holy Spirit. In writing, I have demonstrated to you the norms of the father, the son, and the Holy Spirit. May God direct your understanding to know how to pray and seal your prayer by the help of the Holy Spirit, with whom we stay on earth to work.

Say this prayer with faith.

> God, I believe you exist and created heaven and earth. You gave us your only begotten son, Jesus Christ to die for our sins. I submit myself to the norms of salvation. I believe he resurrected on the third day of his death and went to the father in heaven. May the Holy Spirit, whom he gave to us on earth in the name of your son, take control over my life and guide me to encounter your power to transform my life. Let my enemies read themselves the definition of your transformation by the encounter. Amen!

With faith, this short prayer will raise up a testimony after reading this book. There is a spiritual connection established in everything that faith causes to work, and that connection provokes the flow of virtue from God.

Faith took place there, and an unexpected miracle explored. Jesus said that somebody had tapped into what he carried; somebody had connected with his virtue and had drawn out of him for a change of position. Every time faith comes alive in any area of your life, you connect to divinity, and it is the living word to produce living proof.

In 2 Kings 5: 1–10, Naaman furiously predicted the big, high rivers in Damascus, where he comes from, thinking it would have been better to wash himself there instead of the one in Israel. However, when his servant approached him appealing to his heart to accept the prophetic direction given to him by Elisha, he did it, and the Bible said the flesh was restored like the flesh of a little child, and he was clean. Take note that "Faith is not the mind but the heart". Your mind is not in your vision but your heart, and therefore your heart is needed to perform in the encounter.

Spiritual Preservation: Fasting and Prayer

Encountering the power of God needs a relationship that frequently flows the anointing to attract the emotional conduct of redemption. Spiritual preservation adjusts and ejects the unfaithful daily activities in order to receive vibrant results from God. God is a spirit and works in the spiritual realm. He undertakes his accelerated responsibilities when he is called in holiness. The soul is fed with spiritual strength when it abstains from all ethics of vanity. In fact, the father and the son, who stay in heaven, morally applaud the Holy Spirit's work when the spirit is preserved by a child of God seeking an encounter. I want you to know that searching for the key to your victory is endorsed by God, and the Holy Spirit is assigned to direct you. It is important to meet the right people, read the right books, and attend the right gatherings in order to sense the direction of how to get your key to victory.

Fasting and praying as a manifestation of preserving the spirit creates a great challenge for the kingdom of darkness. It recollects the fundamental originality of your route, and those in positions of authority in the evil kingdom lose and release the trend of your soul because they are attacked by the angels sent by the Holy Spirit. Why does this happens? It is because the Holy Spirit wants to work hand in hand with your soul, and there is no way he can do that in the shadow of the soul.

In 1999 I was worshiping in a church in Ghana when the Holy Spirit visited me. That was where I cried throughout the service, and after church the pastor told me that the Holy Spirit got me out of the world; I had been touched and chosen. Since then I have not done anything without consulting the Holy Spirit, because I came to realise the division of labour in the spiritual assignment of God.

You might be surprised at how powerful it is to preserve your spirit and feed it with prayer. Whether you believe this or not, it is real and you cannot change it. Everybody is limited to his field. God called me and chose me as a teacher, and my duty is to raise up leaders in Christ and preach the gospel in nothing but the truth. I will not use his platform to castigate other men of God; I would rather pray for those using his name to deceive others, so that they might know the light and turn away from their ways. As a result, all my leaders in my ministry have preached the word whenever an opportunity is given to them to mount a pulpit. People in Germany can't believe my ministry is surviving and doing great in the city of Hamburg, but the secret is that when the spirit is preserved, the encounter is unbreakable.

> As they ministered to the lord and fasted, the Holy Spirit said, "Now separate to me Barnabas and Saul for the work to which I have called them." Then having fasted and prayed, and laid his hands on them, they sent them away. (Acts 13: 2–3)

Sacrifice

The world today is based on sacrifices. Everything is based on what you do for reward, and your actions must exceed the expectations in order to be applauded as a significant sacrifice. National leaders fulfil their leadership responsibilities by rewarding civil servants who sacrifice for the good mandates of the nation. Parents reward a son who sacrifices household protection, and organisations reward staff who sacrifice their time for effective operation. The question is, why? It is a strong activism that hits the wall and returns with positive effect and no negative returns.

Moreover, in ages within religious zeal, the mythic origins of the nature of sacrifice actually tell us a great deal about the ritual's manifestation. I want you to understand and to differentiate between the olden days' means of sacrifice and those of today. They did it to resort to belief. According to the legends, the Titan Prometheus was assigned the task of creating the first sacrifice in order to establish the proper relationship between their gods and men once Zeus, a supreme appointed position of authority, had assumed power and distributed authority amongst his siblings. This is a sacrifice to create relationship: he assumes wishes and values. I will continue a bit to let you know about what you sacrifice and what you get. You sometimes promise God on a sacrifice, and obviously you fail. Sacrifice lifts your vision direct to God for a divine encounter. Therefore it plays an important role in cooperating with your inner spirit as you seek to encounter the power of God.

Sacrifice is not about partiality or activism; it is about being pleased by people around you or your environment. It is from the heart, and it takes you deeply but for the sake of beliefs behind the sacrifice. You ignore any negative, persuasive conduct of regrets. What have you been through,. and what have your survived? From your route you are tormented, and by the encounter you have survived because your sacrifice for the Holy Spirit has exceeded the expectation of the Most High God. Don't cheat yourself into thinking that you are fooling God, because God is omnipotent: he knows all things and sees all occurrences, so he cannot be mocked.

The legends of this story in the Greek age, which is all about sacrifice, continues to say that by using a steer, Prometheus hoped to fool the gods by tricking them into taking the worst parts. He wrapped the bones in appealing fat but wrapped the best meat in nasty entrails. Zeus knew it was a trick, but he went ahead and chose the bones anyway – and in the process, he won. Prometheus thought that he was giving out men the best part, but in eating meat they acquired the need to eat it, and at the same time, they had the flaw of mortality. Men were now enjoying the consumption of something dead, which in turn meant that they would die themselves. Gods, however, were content with the pleasant smell of burning bones, fat, and spices, and they retained their immortality and stayed young because they had no direct contact with the corruption of death. Thus, the sacrifice created by Prometheus in order to establish the relationship between gods and men did so in a way that was detrimental to men, despite his best intentions. You see, life with expectation is all about sacrifice. Sow not to please you but to please your God. Sacrifice plays a vital role in your encounter with God; it creates a relationship between you and God, and it's your leverage for experiencing the encounter.

At first our great-grandfathers respected the gods and agreed to human sacrifice. Your son can be used for sacrifice, but now due to salvation, the son of God came to the earth to die for your sins, and you are free and pay the pride of homage. All is no more, but you still find it difficult to sacrifice for your own freedom.

Giving sacrifice, spiritual preservation sacrifice, sowing seed sacrifice, offering sacrifice – all these are common sacrifices for your own good, and they will not be a detriment to your welfare, health, and environment but will strengthen your spirit and purify your soul. It also serves as a weapon of sealing your financial breakthrough so that you may finally have your encounter. I want to prove to you that offering sacrifice can automatically break you through your finances. Human sacrifice probably had a lot to do with social order and maintaining a highly stratified society according to the crafts of the culture and the kingships. Before a king took office, there was probably a sacrifice. I want you to understand that before a throne there should be a sacrifice. Specifically, this history of human sacrifice in the feast of mortality demonstrated here will open your mind to understand and value the salvation brought to you by the son of God, Jesus Christ, who came to die for our sins. All these human sacrifices are now seen to be sacred, and it is not accepted in the kingdom of God.

The Maya lived in subtropical Mesoamerica, in parts of the present-day countries Guatemala, El Salvador, Belize, Honduras, and the Yucatan Peninsula area. The Maya practiced human sacrifice and condoned the motives of the gods. It probably was not because they didn't value human life, but it was an attention to what they believed. On the contrary, they were making a true human sacrifice when they shed blood, and they did so in many forms. Mayan priests used stingray spines and knotted cords to draw blood from their own bodies as offerings to gods, and they made sure it exceeded the pleasant limit of the gods and accelerated their beliefs of redemption.

How do you regard and value your sacrifice to God, and how do you practice it? Does it take blood from your body or a life of a family member? Your answer will tell your cushions how God is good to you, irrespective of your sins. He loves you and is ready to save you from your sins. Sacrifice your life for Christ, and he will shape it to cut all the edges of your problems; your encounter will automatically skip to your vision, and those they never thought of will see you there, though your testimony will change the lives of many.

Sacrifices for God will make you an extraordinary human. It is thought that wars were waged to provide sacrificial victims; providing victims would make the wars more justified. This means all pillars in your life will be broken into pieces as justification of your sacrifice for God. The reasons the Maya gave for their human sacrifices were that they thought their gods resided in people to maintain the order of the universe. They believed that the myth of creation revealed a feathered serpent who brought time from the underworld to humans, and it is feathered and marked with a calendar, human sacrifice, and butlership. The sacrifice was a form of repayment for this gift from the underworld. The Maya may have employed a sympathetic magic in their human sacrifices when they put humans down a well during a drought. You may be surprised about the intents and motives behind sacrifice. You now know how others worked, taking lives and appreciating gods for the defeat of their enemies.

Encountering the power of God is for your own good, and it does not demand human blood, only your commitment to the way of the truth and the life. I think it is a reasonable agenda for the virtue of your life. God is so good to you and does not exchange lives to defeat your enemies. I want you to be aware of how real it was when sacrifice was a major weapon to defeat enemies. Your sacrifice will determine the destination of your vision; sacrifice is the strength you provide in support of your vision, and indeed it is one of the keys to accelerate your encounter with God.

Obedience

Obedience is the power to form a victory, and it marks the critical juncture of your endeavour and contributes to the terminal destruction of the enemies only if it is obedience to the word. It defines the obedience of the commandment of the highest God. God, the maker of heaven and earth, did all things; according to the scripture, he created only man as his own image. This is a very core statement that defines the value of human life, and the only thing that impeaches the most valuable image as he who is man is sinful – and sin is the disobedience of his commandment. This perfectly explains that obedience and disobedience participate effectively either to attract the glory of God to your life, or to make you come up short in your search for that glory.

God told Adam and Eve that they had the right to eat all the fruits in the garden, but this particular one was not for them to eat. God was putting them under the caution of obedience. This meant that from creation, obedience was one of the key practices for man in order to have everlasting life. I was sharing my life experience with a member in my ministry, and after I had gone deep into the story, I couldn't hide my emotions. Before I realised it, I was shedding tears; if I compared it to that of today, it had to be cured by the Most High God. I told him that the key that lifted me to have my encounter with God was obedience. My ministry, now in Hamburg, is among the divine and anointed churches, and I stand as a man of God to declare that the power of obedience may come your way so that you may encounter the power of God.

You are facing a lot of challengers, and a lot of people accusing you because your explanation seems complicated to them. You are confused and dejected, and not every environment accepts you. I am telling you to be obedient and run to God; it is a step that will lift you to meet the encounter, and all these affiliated calamities will be a history which will not be recorded in your good book of episodes, because God has changed your world and has given you the power to change your life.

Chapter 3

What Is Power?

Power is the authority that controls and obligates leadership. It takes effect and controls the outcome in the manner of authority. Power takes effect in both negative and positive ways, depending on the source, the medium, and the destination. If one's life is ruled by power from a negative source, then it deprives pleasure to the victim, and he serves under slavery. When one is controlled by power from the source of vibration from God, then he is redeemed and his heart is full of comfort.

In addition, the correct perceptive principle of life cannot hold when it is not controlled by power, because the power is the spirit that authorizes your obedience and ability to function. That is why you can see a lot of indiscipline activism in various environments: there is a lack of principle of living authorised by power. This happens in our ministries, governments, leadership, firms, and many other areas. Nature existed from the source of power, and power was given to us by God for good use. Satan, who was thrown into the world, has the power to destroy, but if you do not go his way, then you don't fall under the power of his destruction. Satan aims to steal, kill, and destroy everything by the use of his power. He has power to afflict leadership so that he can kill as many people as he wants. He uses the power of complication to ruin lives.

Nations are fighting one another, and people are killed because of power and the influence of political instabilities. Just recently power was commanded, and many lost their lives. This reminds me of just a recent story where a Malaysian flight took off from Amsterdam and headed for Kuala Lumpur, but after it was fifty kilometres from the Ukraine boarder, the Ukraine air controllers lost the flight contact. The following day it was announced to the world that the flight was shot down. May God have mercy upon us. This flight was a civilian flight containing 283 passengers and 15 crew members. Family, friends, children, mothers, and fathers – all of them were lost because of the power one person had at that time, and instead of using it to protect, the power was used for destruction. In this terrible flight disaster, do you know how many people said to their loved ones that they would be back, and yet they never came back?

How do you live your life, and who controls that precious life? A lot of interventions were introduced to support the investigation of the incident, but all of it was corresponding news that was updated every day. We have left God out of all our things we do, both internally and externally, and due to that we strive for no results. The only way to stop all these problems is by encountering the power of God. A nation that seeks the power of God seeks resolution of problems for the entire nation. King Solomon asked for the wisdom of God to be able to attain and keep his leadership responsibilities, and according to the scripture, he was one of the greatest kings the earth has yielded.

Encountering power takes place for effect, and when the practical process is delivered, it is covenanted to create results. Power is not just about dominating; it seeks a required process before it can function. Before it can be respected or disrespected, allowed or disallowed to control, it must rule and control according the norms, ethics, and caution of itself. This connects to a set of rules and obligations to officiate its impact. Power has contributed a lot in the destruction of men, kingdoms, and nations, with the reality of power symbolising creating problems or solving them. In world history, power has contributed to the freedom of mental slavery, yet the same power has also contributed to world wars. This tells you that anything God has made, Satan has fragmented it in the negative way. I therefore appeal to you that the everlasting power of God never harms but prevails the works of redemption, and if you allow yourself to be taken by the power of God, I can promise you that your life will be transformed. Don't be scared about the power of Satan, because when God's power is at work, no power can withstand it. Make sure you seal the covenant with truth and faithfulness, and then the power will work in your life; it will serve as a weapon to defeat the work of the enemies.

> And he said, I saw Satan fall like lightning from heaven, Behold I give you authority to tremble on serpents and scorpions, and over all the power of the enemy and nothing shall be any means shall heart you. (Luke 10: 18–19)

Today I declare and decree in your life that the power of God may come to work in your encounter, in the name of Jesus, the son of the Most High whom I have believed and served. Amen.

Now you can see how power takes effect even in the house of God, portraying in miracles, but the question is what differentiates the good ones from God and the fictitious from the evil? May God open your eyes so that you do not follow the power of destruction and souls are won into the kingdom of Satan.

Now I ask you these questions

1. Who can make a power of God?
2. What minimal provisions does the power of God must contain in order to become legally enforceable?
3. Who can and can't be named as your God in facts?
4. What formalities must be observed when the power of God is at work?

Because of these questions I have asked, it is important to be guided by the Holy Spirit, who lives with you on the earth because there is a basis of spiritual sensitivity that you must acquire to overcome obscure things from the world claiming they are from God. This comes with power, and you might believe it if the Holy Spirit is not in you. You need to be baptised in the Holy Spirit. The Bible said that God he will teach you all things; the Holy Spirit will reveal to you that nobody can make the power of God. Satan cannot make the power of God, but he is an expert in trying to steal, kill, and destroy. That is why it's important to encounter the power of God, because Satan fears it and cannot stand it. Encountering the power of God does not require a qualification in life – it's a simple process, and you will see his power in your domain.

God is supreme, and he created all things. He does not undersign a contract to be permitted before he performs a miracle, and neither does he consult anybody to analyse it. Under no circumstances does he have minimal provisions of his power. This tells you that God's power is above all; he is omnipotent, and he sees and knows everything. In this case, who can and can't be named as your God is important to identify so that you can observe when the power of God is at work versus that of Satan. May the Holy Spirit guide you and teach you all things so that you can know the springing power of Satan versus the durable powers of God. The springing power of Satan is one that only goes into effect if you have allowed yourself into his kingdom, either by sin or by worshiping him; you have become mentally incompetent and spiritually taken by his deeds, and you can no longer properly control yourself because you are taken in the darkness. In fact, your name in a springing power of Satan will not have any legal authority to manage your progression or prosperity unless and until God intervenes to favour you to experience an encounter with him. The main devilish weapon of relying on a springing power of Satan is that it will delay your time of knowing the difference, and your assets and attention in spirit might be taken away. In order to recover, it takes the grace of God. I therefore urge you to be careful, because Jesus said his name will be used to perform miracles, and some will say that they are the son of man, but by their deeds we shall know them.

> All things were made through him, and without him
> nothing was made that were made. In him was life,
> and the life was the light of men, and the light shine in

the darkness and the darkness did not comprehend.
(John 1: 3–4)

A common misconception of unbelievers is that the power of God can perform miracles, but Satan can also perform miracles, so whom should they believe? If a dead man cannot speaks or move, then if you don't have Christ in you, you are similar to a dead man because you are a living dead and have no sensitivity that connects you to see the good and the bad. The sensitivity here symbolizes the work of the Holy Spirit. The fact is that Satan has power in his kingdom, and he can rule you, but only if you make your way into his kingdom. That is why there is a saying that Satan is the ruler of the world; the world here signifies the darkness, so he has power over his kingdom – excluding the children of God. God has power over all; he can take you from the darkness and bring you into the light, and in the light you will have everlasting life. This book specifically teaches you a lot of hidden facts of reality, life, belief, and the power of the encounter. I pray to God to activate the Holy Spirit to assist you in knowing the good way so that you don't follow the evil way and become lost forever.

A member of my ministry asked me how a spirit can be controlled by evil. I told him that the evil spirit first weakens your internal spirit by leading you to sin; he gives you the power to sin and transfer your spiritual ownership of assets after your internal spirit is weak and seems to be dead. Continuous sinning takes you away completely from God, making you come short of the glory of God (Rom. 3: 23). That is where Satan gets leverage over your life. Taking a closer analysis of power defines its own identity, and God is a very powerful ruler, so encountering the power of God results in creating prosperity and accomplishing your vision.

A power encounter is a process one uses to experience a covenant, which is the major key in the process of encountering. It can be a practice, it can be in a form of worship, and it can even be a dialogue. After this is done, you will experience the encounter effect. Encountering with power is something serious because it transmits your spiritual heritage from generation to generation. This means that having an encounter with power is something serious. It rules and dominates your life, and it even affects your children depending on how you formed and sealed it. It is not something you simply come across, because human beings don't just appear on earth without the source of creation. This book will draw your attention to how powerful encountering the living God is, its simplicity of process, and how deadly it is when encountering an evil power. You must choose where you belong.

The majority of the problems of our day is the result of powers our forefathers encountered, which resulted in curses. Every family has a history, and so there is a secret, and it is sacred from the truth. Your mother might tell you what her grandfather told her, and it might be different from what her grandmother explained to her. This means that it has no trace and is a trend of calamities. The only one who can reveal the secret of the encountered covenant is the Most High God. Today as you read this book, I pray by the power of God that every curse must be broken. You need to know how relevant it is to have an encounter with God's power in your life in order to be free from bondage.

Having an encounter with the power is simple, and you might not believe how it works. This book will teach, direct, and lead you to greatness in your encountering with God.

Chapter 4

Power Of The Encounter

In this chapter, God specifically gave me a revelation in the scripture which describes relentless obstacles in prosperity, and how it is dealt with by angelical assistance assigned by the power of God through divine command of authority. There is a strong power in the encounter that manifests against employers of our problems, and it absolutely functions in a mysterious way which is beyond physical understanding of mankind. There are a lot of forces in the spiritual world responsible for controlling and exploring our historic evil covenant. It has a strong array that stands to avert mankind from having salvation, and due to this they operate every second by enhancing their wings to all areas to chase people's destiny into a deep hole. The hole represents prison of life where you can find stagnations, barrenness, disappointment, aggravated poverty, traumatic accidents and so many problems you can think of. This bitterness in life experience generates grieves and rigidity in our heart, and causes a lot of spiritual deprivation such as self control and mind mediation. In our daily life activities, we encounter a lot of hindrances which deprive us from joy in our heart. We fight not with the flesh and physical entities of the world but it is a spiritual battle with demons who at first were angels of God, who sinned and fell with Satan in his rebellion against God. In this case, God himself is aware of demonic operations and then revokes great power in us to go through out the encounter which totally imparts live without the trace of enemies. This determines the task we have been given to accomplish by the help of the Holy Spirit. Encountering the power of God is the salvation of the destiny and deals with the spirit which the Holy Spirit cannot be left out because He lives with us on the earth and teaches us all things.

> (Act1:8)
> *But you shall receive power when the Holy Spirit*
> *has come over you; and you shall be witness to me*
> *"in Jerusalem and in all Judea and Samaria*
> *and to the end of the earth."*

I was overwhelmed after God has revealed to me about how destinies are weeping, shouting and screaming for help. In the revelation, I could see a deep hole where you cannot see the end; total darkness covers the surface of the hole and I was emotionally traumatised and in the dream I asked God, "you are the Almighty and has all power to intervene in situation of mankind so why do you allow the suffering cave spinning right at the door step of your children?" and He said to me. "I have all power to command destinies to come out of satanic holes and trends, I created heaven and earth including man as my own image but why has man forsaken me? I am the creator of all things and I have power to command all things but man has chosen to live in his own ways". This revelation to me really describes the pains that endure in the heart of the creator that for man denying the purpose of creation and rejection of His word through consultation of idols and advise from the ordinary anti-evolutionist. God is merciful that he protects us and gives us life. God referred me to Peter's experience

(Peter freed from prison).

Act 12:5-11
"Peter was therefore kept in prison but constant prayer
was offered to God for him by the church. And when
Herod was about to bring him out, that night peter
was sleeping bound with two chains between two soldiers;
and guards before the door were keeping the prison.
Now behold, an angel of the lord stood by him
and a light shone in the prison; and he struck peter on
the side and raised him up, saying, "Arise quickly!"
And his chain fell off his hands then the angel said to him .
"Gird yourself and tie on your sandals", and so he did.
And he said to him "and put on your garment and follows me,
So he went out and follows him, and did not know that what
was done by the angel and was real but though, he was seeing a vision
When they were past the first and the second guard posts,
they came to the Iron gate that leads to the city,
which opened to them of its own accord; and they went out
and went down one street, and immediately the angel
departed from him, and when peter has come to himself, he said,
"Now I know for certain that the lord has sent His angel
and has delivered me from the hands of Herod and
from all the expectations of the Jewish people."

Now you could realise that after you have acquired the entire spiritual directive, you achieve defeats of the enemies that transgress upon you. This takes effect spiritually where your soul comes in contact with the Holy Spirit assisting you to meet the encounter. God, therefore, undertake his covenant responsibility between man and himself, and fulfilled his promise to man that He owns all power and his power is above all and his protection is under his feet. God then shoots out extraordinary power to free you from bondages through the assistance of an Angel (Angelical assistance). According to the bible, Peter experienced the encounter which was manifested by the powerful command of God and angel appeared from heaven to release Peter out of prison. Peter's experience in comparison to current lives symbolises where Satan has kept our destiny and how the power in the encounter can command destiny to be moved out of that prison. I was once in my office in the church when a man visited me, he said to me, "Pastor I have a testimony which I want to share with you because I am overwhelmed and I don't know how to express myself concerning what I saw". I sat well to listen to him because I could see from his eyes that he has encountered something which he finds it very difficult to understand. He continued by saying "Pastor, before last night I said to God that for 8 years now that I lost my job and everything I acquired through my effort, I asked God why is it that I run all my ways to follow him but I still face problems one after the other, according to him, he felt asleep whiles praying. He had a dream that two men in white came to him and said to him, "brother, here is a book which we want to confirm your written name in it; it is a book of life which contains names of great people who were able to keep the faith and won the race. It is a book with names of only those with the garment that glow in purity, those pure in heart". He continued flipping pages of the book and the pages couldn't finish. Then one said to him, "your works are not yet done for salvation, seek first his kingdom and the rest shall be given unto you".

He woke up from the dream and saw all his cloth wet. Since then he worked on his salvation and threw away all his intents of wealth recovery. This then became leverage for his encounter. Some months after, he had the dream that the same two men were changing his cloth, his shoes and they held him out of a broken gate. I was surprise of his dream because it was very similar to the story of Peter in the Bible who was arrested and kept in prison. You see, God has a core mandate for an angel to guide you out of your problems. You might not have a dream but spiritually God will see to your situation only if you will have faith and understand his face of encounter where seeking for salvation is the key to open the tale of redemption .

PRISON IN OUR LIVES SIMPLIFIES THE FOLLOWING

1. Prison serves as a place of troubles and bondages in our lives.
2. Prison serves as a place of confusion.
3. Prison serves as sorrow and pains which cause emotional traumatised
4. Prison is a place of darkness where life could never be established. You can never establish life in darkness.
5. Prison describes dangerous zone where memories hunt joy and replace it with fear.

Peter's days ahead of him were absolutely unpredictable and he was facing an obstructive barrier that separates him from his exploration. Sometimes, you wonder why you cannot shine and share out divine testimonies to motivate others because you could see that you have what it takes to boast of and nothing seems to function; it is a sign of your life being kept in prison. There are many situations that hold us stagnant in mind, thinking that God has forsaken us; likewise when human effort has failed, and hopes are diminished, accusations and persecutions then separate memories of motivation from belief.

Peter was physically dejected but when power manifested in the encounter, the light shone in the prison; it was a sudden light from heaven and an angel of the lord appeared to assist him. May God show you His light in your encounter with Him. It is my prayer that since you have set the target of receiving Him as your personal saviour, doing away with your sins, I challenge your enemies that your life will never be in their hands henceforth because the light has shone to cover the darkness as prison in your life.

EFFECT OF THE POWER IN THE ENCOUNTER (GOD'S LIGHT)

God has so many ways of rendering services of intervention. He uses His authority to deprive pleasure and desire of our enemies and in His Presence, every curse and every covenant are broken, and His power invokes command to establish immediate results. This occurs to all things that might be at stake of life prosperity or deliverance. This is natural in the effect when power is dominated in the encounter. When generations encounter God they come face to face with perfect favour and things begin to happen in mysterious ways. The effect of God's power has a special role to play in encounter with God. I strongly believe that most of our problems are taken on by surprise because we sometimes don't really know how it happened. Invariably, God sometimes takes Satan by surprise through a command which immediately takes effect to release miracle under his power of authority. The effect of the power of God spiritually holds control in a format of reforming lives of mankind. The effect of the power of God rendered a control in a divine format which reformed Jerusalem

> Isaiah 52:1-2
> *Awake, awake! Put on your strength, O Zion*
> *O Jerusalem, the holy city! For the uncircumcised*
> *and unclean shall no longer come to you, shake*
> *yourself from the dust, arise; Sit down, O Jerusalem!*
> *Lose yourself from the bonds of your neck,*
> *O captive daughter of Zion*

There are two things that work as effect in the power that manifests in the encounter, that is, recovery and restoration. In so many chapters in the scriptures, there are evidences of recovery and restoration and they never stand on their own but they walk with the enforcement of the power of God. This enhances the glory because testimonies are derived and shared to motivate the dead souls to set a target to encounter the power of God. This fact has really yield my ministry a strong evangelical team that performs great in preaching the gospel to lives without hopes which makes me realise that life recovery and restoration is in the hand of the creator because He only gives life. Now you could realise that the power has all the spiritual right to put you in line of your encounter as a significant of its effect which serves as the source of testimonies.

THE MAJOR KEYS EFFECT OF THE POWER IN THE ENCOUNTER

1. The effect of the power rise you up; it revives you from a broken soul and gives you hope.
2. The effect of the power breaks chains from your hands.
3. The effect of the power authorises shameful cloth to disappear. The shameful cloth symbolises the story which makes people rejected you and disappoint you. With that cloth, you are consider as outcast who is shameless and disgrace to the city.
4. The effect of the power replaces your shameful cloth with a new beautiful garment. This signifies that God changes your story and gives you new identity, favour, hope and everlasting life.
5. The effect of the power grants you an anointing motion in new shoes: A shoe that walks you away from problems, treading path and possession of the enemies.
6. The Iron Gate opens for your trespassing.

I point to you directly that if it is not the power in the encounter, these life dissertations can never be broken and like wise by the power in the encounter things beyond can be broken. The main focus of the heart is to acquire faith in his power, it is the leverage we discover from the process of encountering the power of God, so you can see that God is very wise to sustain you in his medium array of destination where he leads you out of your problems because His empowerment in your encounter is to take back what the devil has stolen from you. Satan, the deceiver is vigorously opposing God and therefore a war arose in spirit and Satan is the loser. This is all about our sins that draw us closer to the enemy yet God intervenes because the blood of Jesus has paid for that. I sometimes wonder how others conduct research and value sacrifice on the second part of the ministry of Christ which is the suffering of the son of God. It is my prayer that God will continue to have mercy upon our souls and He who sees everything shall draw us closer to meet His power to clear our ways from evil. The Power of God does not compromise with the enemy, it does not come timidly, nor does it come apologetically, it comes in power.

Moses challenged the gods of Egypt and never compromised with them because he had the power to defeat them. God spoke to Moses and revealed to him the power in his command and gave him instruction according to his words. Elijah challenged the prophets of Baal on Mount Carmel. All these power encounters in the Old Testament served to show Israel and the pagan people that Jehovah is the only God worthy of our service and worship. Let us therefore give praise to His Name for His salvation and authority given to us against enemies that stands our way.

(Exodus 7:3)
" *And I will harden Pharaoh's heart, and multiply*
My signs and My wonders in the land of Egypt but
Pharaoh will not heed you, so that I may lay My
hand on Egypt and bring My armies and My people,
the children of Israel out of the land of Egypt by great
judgement" .

POWER OF THE MESSAGE IN THE ENCOUNTER

(Isaiah 53:1-5) NIV
Who has believed our message?
And to whom has the arm of the lord been revealed?
He is despised and rejected by men
A man of sorrows and Aquitaine with grief
And we hide, as it were, our faces from him
He was despised and we did not esteemed him
Surly he was born our grief And carried our sorrow;
Yet we esteemed him stricken, Smitten by God, and afflicted

But he was wounded for our transgression,
He was bruised for our iniquities;
The chastisement for our peace was upon him,
And by his stripes we are healed.

The power of God carries a weapon which is the word that illustrates "message". It invokes instant release of extra ordinary power and portrays positive results when man has face to face encounter with God. It is then very important to know the role which the word plays in the encounter and I have specifically emphasised the motive behind the message(gospel) which is the birth, crucifixion and the resurrection of Jesus Christ because it holds the definition of the message which is the power in the encounter. The Word is the light that shines on you to sustain your life contact efficiency with God; the relation between you and God is approved by the Word and connects you to receive your redemptive right as a son of God. Jesus Christ, the son of God, who came to the earth to die for our sins had the anointing of preaching the Word and through that we have salvation. He never lost concentration neither did He lose sight of His father; He was always closer to God, and Satan was also undertaken his role to cause deviation of the mission of Christ but by the power in the Word, Jesus was able to stand to meet His accomplishment. The message in the encounter qualifies you no matter your sins you have committed, you can be saved and you will be guided the Holy Spirit who we live with us now on earth. This stands for faith for a man to know that he can be saved and have everlasting life.

I want to reveal a secret to you today and may you understand with faith. Whenever you encounter the power of God, you receive message as a directive from God through dreams, visions, hearing and most, through the word. It is therefore your secret to your success which needs to be worked on by the guidance of the Holy Spirit. Your physical appearance will get your enemies confuse and they will never understand. Sometimes it is obvious to render a prove of your transformation but yet your enemies will not understand and will never be able to know the source but he who has granted you his favour secures you knowledge to understand and work with it. That is why when Jesus was dying on the cross, he shouted and spoke to his maker but the people who witnessed his death with joy didn't understand what he was saying.

(Matthew 27:45)
Now from the sixth hour until the ninth hour
there was darkness over all land.
About the ninth hour Jesus cried out with a loud voice,
saying "Elli Eli,lama sabachtanai "that is "My God ,
My God why have you forsaken me"?!
Some of those who stood there, when they heard that, said,

> *"This man is calling Elijah!". Immediately one of them
> ran and took a sponge,*
> *filled it with sour wine and put it on a reed and offered
> to Him to drink.*
> *The rest said "let him alone; let us see if Elijah will come
> to save him."*
> *And Jesus cried out again and with a loud voice, and
> yielded his spirit.*

May your message received from God in your encounter confuse your enemies in Jesus name!

After man has set up a target over his circumstances to have encounter with God, he is divinely directed by the Holy Spirit to receive remission of his sins because he has believed in Him who is the son of God and has also believed in the death and resurrection of the son of God. Indeed, it is written in the bible that whosoever believes in him shall not perish but have everlasting life. This belief is a spiritual transformation of life from the world into his kingdom because the resurrection of Jesus Christ is the indication of his dominion over Satan's kingdom which serves as demonstration of his Power.

The message on the cross is the salvation which deals with the resurrection of Jesus Christ for mankind to have encounter with God, the message becomes the object guide to lead man towards salvation which is the tale redemption of destiny. The message gets you understand salvation as the basic tool and guide to have you contact with the encounter. Therefore the message operates for man to know and understand the reason of the birth of Jesus Christ, the crucifixion and the resurrection .He came to carry the sorrow and he was wounded for our transgression and his blood was spilled for our sins to be forgiven by the father.

Many of our days have met the preliminary consideration of the encounter through the message that carries the power to heal. This refers to a ministry encounter which is a manifestation where God gives out divine message to a minister to use to heal the sick and cast out demons. When a minister approaches such a ministry encounter, it is essential that he gives serious consideration to the healing environment through the power in the message. It is then important to know the relevance of the message in the encounter. Jesus after that he was filled with power, He went about doing good and healing all who were oppressed by the devil for God was with Him. It is then an encounter of men who believes in Him through the message which is the word.

> (Acts 10:43)
> *"To him all the prophets witness that, through*
> *His name whoever believes in Him*
> *will receive remission of sins"*

Man has a distance with God, and that is where the power of the "message" exposes to manifest. God always wants to speak to man but our sins prevent his presence that is why He said "for all have sin and they have come short of the glory of God (Roman 3:23). Whenever there is short of the glory on us, it simply describes the distance between us and God.

THE EFFECT OF POWER OF THE MESSAGE IN THE ENCOUNTER

1. The power in the message heals the sick
2. The power in the message can change the history in your family
3. The power in the message can cause transformation of life
4. The power in the message can cause revelation to understand His ways
5. The power gives adequate guide to exemption of sacred satanic rebellions.
6. The message enhances wisdom to obey God.
7. The message resurrects our destiny to function because His resurrection validated his dominion over satanic kingdom.
8. The message in the power of encounter transforms the heart to love God. This automatically defeats Satan.

MESSAGE AS A COMMAND IN THE ENCOUNTER

(Act 9:1)

Saul still breathing threats and murder against
the disciples of the lord. Went to the high priest,
and asked letter from him to the synagogues of
Damascus so that if he found any who were on
the Way, whether men or woman, he might bring
them bound to Jerusalem. As he journeyed,
he came near Damascus and suddenly a light was
shone around him from heaven
Then fell to the ground, and head a voice saying to him
"Saul, Saul, why are you persecuting me?"

And he said,"who are you, Lord?"
then the lord said "I am Jesus ,whom you are persecuting,
it is hard for you to kick against the goads"
So he, trembling and astonished, said "lord what do
you want me to do?" Then the lord said to him
"Arise and go into the city, and you will be told what
you must do."

The motive behind our encounter is to seek for God's intervention to restore lives which have been kept under covenants invoked by our current atrocities and that of our ancestors. It is also the determination we engage to attain prosperity, therefore, God attests a significant power of command against enemies after us. That is why He said that He has all power to stand against all principalities, and commanding protection in the encounter becomes the redemptive right entitled to by mankind. The power exploration is the command he exercises to cast demons from our way of surviving in the face of encounter. There are so many satanic spirits that fight you to meet the power manifestation in the encounter and the spirits who are in-charge of such operating along your process of meeting the encounter are the demons and the only way to deal with demons is to cast them out by the power in a form of command. God uses power of command to cast them out our ways,

Demons are truly strong spirits who are against our prosperity, they are indeed agents of darkness who operate with many combinations of forces to attack us especially when we are on target to encounter the power of God, but God is a faithful God who always fulfils his promise. He stands and fights for our redemption.

(Matthew 25: 41)
Then he will also say to those on the left hand,
depart from me, you cursed, into the everlasting
fire prepared from he devil and his angels.

Demons are probably angels who sinned and fell with Satan in his rebellion against God so you can imagine the origination which describes what power they have but God is above all and has power to cast them out. (Revelation 12:9). Demons are powerful spirits they operate against progression and success, and encounter brings reformation of lives when one meets the power of God. Satanic rebellion never seeks for the deployment of your released destiny that is why they are considered to be morally perverted and evil. It is likely that demons enter into people purposely to destroy them and to destroy others, and that is what I describe as territorial spirit, and its take the command in the power to cast out such demons. There are territorial spirits who sometimes enter into people to destroy especially mass number of people who are followers of Christ. These are demons who hold controls and influence not over individuals, but also over certain localities, people, groups, societies and churches but when the command in the power of God manifest those demons are cast out and God can use such victims to preach his Word and win souls for his kingdom. Saul was in the act of territorial spirit who stood against the disciples of the lord; he killed the followers of Christ. Saul went to the high priest, and asked for letter from him to the synagogues of Damascus so that if he found any who was on the Way, whether men or woman, he might bring them bound to Jerusalem. What do you think and why was he persecuting God's people, and under what circumstances will he kill the followers of Christ? There is something you must know about the power in the Word and its circulations. Demons cannot stand against the Word; they rather fight against spiritual employees of the Word. I am talking about those who preach the word .There is no way Satan can attack the Word but he can attack the preachers of the Word and the recipients of the Word. Saul was opposing the name of Jesus; he breathed threats and murder against the disciples of the lord. He was a man who truly hated Christ and all who were associated to him. The power of God threw his sudden light to Saul when he was on his way closer to Damascus, through that Saul became blind for three days and ate nothing within those days; Saul was healed through the power in the message given to Ananias.

When ever God's power is manifested in a form of an encounter, there is a revelation which holds a message for a specific assignment;

- restoration your life back to its original form
- revelation of understanding God's power
- revelation to understand the vision of God
- to know and understand your dignity
- To know your divine purpose of assignment
- Yoke upon shoulders may be broken

A revelation was given to Ananias and the revelation was containing a powerful message which assigned Ananias to perform a miracle to Saul. He said, "I am sent to lay my hands upon you so that you may see again and be filled with the Holy Spirit" Saul received his sight at once and he arose and was baptised and there came to him the wind of supernatural. So when he had received food, he was strengthened .Saul spent days with the disciples as a form of reconciliation and is the union between the falling and the divine. This is the reign of peace when ever there is a recovery and transformed by the power of God

IMPARTATION BY LAYING ON OF HANDS

The bible said when Ananias laid his hands on Saul, there was an impartation; a "SCALE" was removed from his eyes and he could see again. This was a spiritual power acceleration which caused a divine change.

(Saul converted through the encounter)

1. The veil was removed.
2. The curse was broken.
3. Confusion was dissolved.
4. The damage was restored.
5. He could see again.

OUR REDEMPTIVE RIGHT IN THE ENCOUNTER

Redemption simply means ransom. Historically, according to definitions from many Christian authors, redemption was used in reference to the purchase of slaves for freedom, that was when a slave was redeemed, that is when a price was paid for his freedom. God spoke about Israel's deliverance from slavery in Egypt and it was a task which was to be achieved by a divine guidance. He said that I am the lord, and I will bring you out from the burdens of the Egyptians and I will deliver you from slavery. I will redeem you with an outreached arm and with great act of judgment. This illustrates put up how redemption is important to the creator, and how needed it is to man but the anticipation of corporation with the process of redemption has now been the problem to man and I wonder why we sacrifice to be slaves but not to be redeemed. Redemption is a purchased back of something that has been lost, and there are instances that define the lost of our freedom and God has laid down his own to bring back the lost as our right we receive from his face of encounter.

(Exodus 6:6) the use of the redemption in the New Testament includes the same idea. Every person is a slave to sin; only through the price Jesus paid on the cross is a sinful person redeemed from sin and death. Every person stands in need of redemption because everybody has sinned (Roman 3:23). We are justified by his grace as a gift through redemption that is in Christ Jesus and is he the mediator of new covenant since death has occurred that redeemed us from the transgression committed under the first covenant.

Redemption has a great definite role in our encounter with God which is the freedom for believers who have attain the remission of sins from the cross. Some benefits of the redemption right when man has encounter with God include: forgiveness of sin

(Ephesians 1:7), eternal life (John 3:16), peace with God (colossians1:18-20) have the holy spirit in us (1 Corinthians 6:19-20).

These benefits stand for our redemption right when man has experienced the encounter because when we are redeemed, we become different people. We attain the divine close distance to God through Jesus Christ, and in Him we have new identity because he paid a high price for our redemption. The ultimate sacrifice of his own life freed us from sin.

> (Revelation 5:9-12)
> *"And they sang a new song saying*
> *You are worthy to take a scroll*
> *And to open it seals; for you wear slain*
> *And have redeemed us O God by your blood*
> *Out of every tribe and tongue and people and nation*
> *And have made us kings and priests to our God*
> *And we shall reign on the earth."*
> *Then I looked, and heard the voice of many angels*
> *Around the throne, the living creature, and the elders,*
> *And the number of them was ten thousand times ten thousand*
> *and thousands of thousands.*

STEPS OF REDEMPTIVE RIGHT THROUGH THE ENCOUNTER

1. He received for us power

He did not need power but he received for us power. This is power that we are entitled to as His children to be able to sustain our encounter with the father. It is then greatness god placed in us for the enemies to submit themselves to us

> (Psalm 66:3)
> *Say to God*
> *"How awesome are your works!*
> *Through the greatness of your power*
> *Your enemies shall submit themselves to you."*

2. He received for us riches.

Jesus became poor so that we might become rich. He was a rich man but due to the redemption, there was a divine exchange of poverty and riches. These constitute the value of his sacrifice and it differentiates riches of the world and that of the spirit.In spirit we are rich because our father owns all riches.

3. He received for us wisdom

He received us wisdom as weapon to reach our destination. Wisdom showed them their way to go after they have left Egypt and according to the bible, pharaoh pursued the even to the red sea. God's wisdom gave a direction to Moses and they crossed the sea without a bridge. By the blood, we are entitled to wisdom which is always available to overcome confusion in life, though I have emphasised how wisdom is applied as a power to seal your encounter but participates here as our redemptive right and the power we have to fight enemies to retain our encounter

> (Proverbs 24:3-4)
> *Through wisdom a house is built*
> *And by understanding it is established;*
> *By knowledge the rooms are filled with all*
> *Precious and pleasant riches*

4. He received for us strength

As they journeyed through the wilderness to Cannan, none among their tribe was feeble but by the blood of Jesus, strength was their portion in the journey. For those who have received the lord Jesus, He is a source of strength for them.

Jesus is full of Grace, and this Grace is always sufficient for us. The Grace makes perfect in our weaknesses.

> (Psalm 110:1-2)
> *The lord said to my lord,*
> *"Sit at my right hand,*
> *I will make your enemies your footstool"*
> *The lord shall send the rod of your strength out of Zion*

5. He received for us honour

Through Jesus Christ, we have received honour which Satan knows it is one of our greatest elements that soul inherited to rejoice. This redemption right provokes Satan a lot because he always wants to see us in pains and sorrow. Israelites found themselves in a desert where there was no food but God released man from heaven and gave them water from the rock to drink. It was not just man's ordinary demonstration because he has power but it is a redemptive right which Jesus has fought on the cross for us.

6. He received for us Glory

We have been justified by the blood to live the glorious life because he received for us honour and glory and due to that no one can despise or cause us rejection. The glory contains power to resist power of condemnation. You can now imagine how you are ordained as a spiritual conqueror. Jesus paid the price for your liberty and no one has the right to take that from you. The price guarantees a glorious life only if you decide to turn your ways into the light.

(I Corinthians 6:20)
For you were bought at a price;
therefore glorify God in your body and in your spirit,
which are God's.

Sometimes, you wonder why your destination on a task does not come with success and you find yourself in failure, that is where you get yourself confuse and start to cure your own task. Don't forget that he has received us the power of the blood to challenge occurrences only if you have believed in him then your redemption right is endorsed to call in glorious assistance from the blood of Jesus. The blood serves as your receipt of purchase and there is no attack of the devil that can cross the blood line.

7.   He received for us blessing

The bible said that God has blessed us with every spiritual blessing in the heavenly place before the foundation of this world, and to be blessed means to be empowered to succeed so by the virtue of the fact that you are a Christian, you are empowered to make in life. On the day of Pentecost the Holy Spirit came upon them to activate all the unlisted redemptive right as the blessing we receive from believing him. The Holy Spirit now lives with us, teach and direct us in all things.

(John 20:19-21)
Then ,the same day at evening being the first day of
the week when the doors were shut where the disciples
were assembled, for fear of the jews, Jesus came and
stood in the Midst, and said to them again peace to you !
As the father he sent Me. I also send to you .
"When he has said this, he showed them his hands

> *and his side, then the disciples where glad when*
> *they saw the lord. So Jesus said to them "peace to you!*
> *As the father has sent me, I also send you."*
> *And when he said this, he breathed on them,*
> *and said to them, receive the Holy Spirit*

This is the turning point setting up a role for the holy spirit .Jesus never left us alone he sent the holy spirit to be with us on the earth I therefore stand by his word I have believed that henceforth ;

> *Every yoke of poverty and nakedness is broken*
> *I destroy every yoke of weakness*
> *I destroy the yoke of shame and I embrace dignity and integrity*
> *I destroy the yoke of sorrow and depression and confusion*
> *I stand by the word, may salvation reach your destination.*
> *In Jesus name I pray. Amen !*

Chapter 5

The Secret Place

After attaining the redemptive right as the son of God, your destiny is secured and preserved under the shadow of the most high as the secret place where perseverance form God takes effect and honor you with endurance and protection. In our normal life, whenever one is consider being important in the society, that is where a set of security guides are created and implemented for his or her safety and such security encodes with method of hiding that person from being harmed because he or she is needed and his life must be preserved. His area of residence is kept clean and expensive and quality materials are used to beautify the place to render comfort service to his presence. The victim is served and being taken care of by special trained staffs but one thing that you must know is that with this security yet his safety is not guaranteed. You cannot compare protection of man to that of the Most High God. You encounter the power of protection under his shadow which is the secret place for your protection. Secret place in your encounter intensifies your protection under his feet and preserved you with his feathers and that is the protection you have against multitude of enemies.

There are so many attacks that arise in the spirit to put away the incentives you are connected to as a believer who has witnessed the encounter. That is why temptations always fall on both side in our everyday life but God has given us his promise of protection at his secret place so no matter the effort of the enemy, none shall come near us. The secret place is considered to be the repository of your destiny where all blessings and progressions are preserved which define the standard of God's establishment around you. It is a promise He has made to us and surely He abides by His promise; it is rather unto us to put up a challenge to dwell in the secret place of the Most High God. It is a place that you can lay hold of the promise.

Moses wrote Psalm 91 as he dwelt in the secret place of the Most High God, in the midst of the dark clouds, it was a place of sacred and holy habitation. The thick clouds are "hiding places" for Moses and he experienced the presence of the Most High, and this is the truth that one who "abides" in the secret place of Most High God dwells in an ascended place of rest –being lifted high and above surrounding. The spiritual compliance of man through faith is important in the encounter because under his shadow, a lot of miracles happen and it takes faith to receive them. The first step to experience the supernatural is to have faith in the power of the encounter because the secret place is the secured place where God reveals his power to perform miracle. The bible explained that no man sees God and lives (Exodus 33:20) so God allow Moses to see his glory only from the secret place.

(Exodus 33:22). God said that when my glory passes by, I will put you in a cleft in the rock and cover you with the hand until I have passed by. Here, God has given us a clue about what we must do to experience the presence of God which could only be enjoyed at the secret place.

THE VALUE OF THE SECRET PLACE

(Psalm 91:1-5)
He who dwells in the secret place of the most
high shall abide under the shadow of the almighty
I will say of the lord" he is my refuge and my fortress
my God in him I will trust." Surely he shall deliver you
from the snare of the fowler, and from the perilous pestilences.
He shall cover you with his feathers, and under his wings
you shall take refuge, His truth shall be your shield and buckler,
you shall not be afraid of the terror by night.

Since secret place remains to be a lovely and protected place, the endurance of his love and protection continues to avail in His promise. God continues to invite us to his secret place not to just experience the grace and leave but to stay with him so he can share his love with us. Dwelling with him in the secret place is a call which is a must for us to neglect the clamour and dirt of the world. Specifically, I want you to know the conditions attached to the invitation to the secret place that is "dwell" which means to "stay" or "live". It is an encounter which lasts forever to transmit your everlasting protection by the power of the Most High God. He encourages man by the norms and ethics of the secret hold of his promises and has given divine characteristics to the secret place where he invite us to dwell in there.

(Gen 28:10-18)

Now Jacob went out from Beersheba and went towards Haran
So he came to a certain place and stayed there
all nigh because the sun had set .And he took one of
the stones of that place and put it at his head, and he
lay down in that place to sleep
Then he dreamed, and behold a ladder was set
up on earth ,and it top reached to heaven and there
the angels of god were ascending and descending on it
And behold the lord stood above it and said
"I am the lord God of Abraham your father and the
God of Isaac ;
the land on which you lie I will give to you and your descendent
Also your descendant shall be as the dust of the earth,
you shall spread abroad to the west and the east ,
to the north and to the south ;and in your seed all the
families of the earth shall be blessed.
Behold I am with you and will keep you wherever you will go,
and I will bring you back to this land for I will not
leave you until I have done what I have spoken to you
The Jacob awoke from his sleep and said.
"surley the lord is in this place ,and I did not know it"
And he was afraid and said. "How awesome is this place !
This is none other than the house of god and this is the
gate of heaven!"

From the above quotation you can glean matured divine characteristics of the secret place which will forever resort you heart not to be trembled of any situation getting you executed because he has given us his promise and we bear the right of redemption; the secret place is a place where you can experience the 4 most spiritual redemptive functions

1. A place of supernatural
2. A place of transformation
3. A place of revelation
4. A place of refuge
5. A place of Devine Encounter

The need to create a close distance communication with your faith is very important when you set up a single minded focus to encounter the power of God because it holds your spiritual sensitivity to be well connected to the Holy Spirit.

This happens in our normal circumstances where believers sometimes are rescued from a terrible situation as sign of God's presence but yet we wonder how such miracle happened. The greatest barrier to the manifestation of supernatural is not demon because demon cannot step in the ways of the supernatural but it is the lack of faith as a believer that brings barrier between the supernatural and its manifestation

The greatest hindrance to the receiving the supernatural is not witch craft power but is the state of naturalness and the bible specifically states that, natural man does not receive the things of the spirit of God for they are foolishness to him; nor can he know them ,because they are spiritually discerned.(I Corinthians 2: 14).

The secret place must be understood in spirit, it is a place of your encounter where he has given us his hold of promises and it manifestation takes place in spirit for those who has faith and has believed to receive his supernatural manifestation. Faith and belief constitute the establishment of experiencing the supernatural in the secret place. I have emphasise much on faith in the processing of encountering the power of God and it holds much efficiency to get closer to determination, it deals with the heart reception of the spirit likewise the secret place holds the norms of exploring through the heart of faith we have to dwell in the secret place.

FAITH AS A KEY TO GET HOLD TO THE SECRET PLACE

(Mark 5:27,28,29,31,34)
*When she heard about Jesus Christ she cam behind
Him in the crowd and touched his garment
For she said, if only I may touch his cloth I shall be made well.
Immediately, the fountain of her blood was
dried up, and she felt in her body that she was healed of affliction.
And Jesus knowing immediately in him self that power
had gone out of him .turned around in the crowd and
said "who touched my cloth"
And he looks at her who had done this thing.
But the woman, fearing, and trembling knowing what
had happened to her, came and fell down before Him
and told Him the whole truth
And He said to her" Daughter, your faith has made you well,
Go in peace and be healed of your affliction."*

Faith is the array of the best insight here in the story of this poor woman who has been troubled with a blood flow for twelve years but just one day she found herself in an old environment where she normally sits and lament. This was transformed into the surface of anointing as a "secret place" where miracle could take place. This impression she had was not an ordinary self-impression but she believed her environment has been transformed and circulated by the power of God and for that thought, faith has already been established, and whenever faith is established, miracle and breakthrough take place. The secret place owns power of transformation where lives carried away by the devil are restored and preserved and has significance of changing environment by supplying it with anointing. I was in a crusade held in Amsterdam by Benny Hinn. I travelled from Hamburg to witness the occasion and when I got to the environment, I felt the motion of the Holy Spirit, and I said to myself "this is the environment of the secret place". Indeed, the occasion was controlled and directed by the anointing, and Benny Hinn's movement across our sitting area rendered a serious sensation where I could feel that the ground was shaking and instant miracles and breakthrough started happening. Due to this personal experience, I strongly believe that the woman with the issue of blood experienced similar presence of the anointing when Jesus was passing and based on that she said "if only I may touch his cloth " that was a fount of faith which led to acquisition of miracle.

The appearance of Jesus Christ describes the presence of the lord and it defines "Secret Place" where the healing stream flows.

Faith gives you the mandate to value the secret place and get hold of his promises therefore gleaning from your belief towards the secret place must equally move with faith because that is the secret which God throw onto you as a challenge of his power contact.

> *(Mark 7:25-28)*
> *For a woman whose young daughter had an unclean*
> *spirit heard about Him to cast out the demons out of*

> *her daughter. and she came and fell at his feet ,and she*
> *kept asking him to cast the demons out of her daughter .*
> *But Jesus said to her " let the children be filled*
> *first, for it is not good to take the children's*
> *bread and throw it to the little dogs."*
> *And the woman answered and said to Him .*
> *"yes lord, even the little dogs under the table*
> *eats from the children's crumbs.*
> *Then he said to her "for this saying go your way,*
> *the demons has gone out of your daughter ."*

The crumbs were described valuable in the secret place through establishment of faith and demons were cast out. I want you to understand the principle that offers you a great miracle at the secret place because many who have set out to achieve and prosper in the secret place testify by embracing faith as the main step key to dwell in the secret place.

If through faith, the description given to crumbs cast out demons in the secret place then through faith your story in the public ugly episode will be changed and things falling on the wrong ways will be redirected to right ways and miracles, breakthroughs and divine favour remain to be your portion in the secret place.

Chapter 6

Why Have an Encounter with God

Lives have been ruined and dumped into the pitch of darkness because of the world's implementation of policies, procedures, and innovations around the world today. Crimes and so many social vices have been in the headlines across the world. This defines the retribution of the world's reliable policies, which forsake God's intervention and power. God said, "Let us make man in our own image, according to our likeness; let them have dominion over the fish of the sea, over the birds of the air, and over the cattle and over all the creep on the earth." This means man encountered God's favour from the beginning of creation, and so you have power over all things on earth. However, your sins and ignorance take you away from God, and you gradually fall under the shelter of darkness, making you to come short of the glory of God.

Intelligence deceives the heart of the foolish, who make decisions without thinking about who owns creation, and this has led to a lot into misery and bondage. In the spiritual world, Satan confines those with weak souls and takes them into the kingdom of darkness. Why have you accepted Satanic philosophy spread across the world, when your knowledge is your God, and by your knowledge you think you can succeed without God's interference? Indeed, the liar with a toxic tongue succeeds by getting a lot into his world, but greater is he who created heaven and earth and all things, and who said, "Let there be light." The light is the truth, and the truth is the word. By the word you shall be set free.

Encountering the reality of life defines nature, which is the origin of everything. There are so many ways you can use it as a tool to solve your problems, but you must be able to identify the required tool. It is obvious that your mind betrays your thinking strength, and you forget about the natural required tool to all problems, which is the power of God. The world now has forsaken God, and it bears the calamites and atrocities because it's a great sin to forsake God. See Romans 3: 23.

The world's bleeding matters to every single person, because if a war is declared, no one can sympathize, and individuals and nations will be washed away. I ask myself if a nation comes short of the glory of God, what happens to those who live within it? Encountering the power of God resolves all situations and controls your redemption. The high rate of world ignorance of God's power has paved the way for Satan to rule the world, and it is a curse to victims because agents of impeaching God existence can affect you and afflicts your success in life. Specifically, I want you to know why we need to encounter the power of God. It does not only have to do with individual prosperity but also the entire world's refreshing and supernatural zeal acceleration. Due to this, the major concept that affects the world in the area of man's definition of God's existence has brought a lot of curses onto the world, and it takes an encounter with God to be free from the curse.

If your biological father denies you as a son and runs away from his core responsibilities, how would you take it if the future granted you a favour, and he came back to help? This is similar to the world's relationship with the creator. The world is bleeding and is living in prison of its own creation. Our intellectual legitimacy has denied God's existence, and it takes the encounter of God to be free from the world's tremendous situations. It is absolutely a curse if we have the notion that God does not exist. You therefore need the encounter of God in order to be part of his children, who have sought the light of protection and have had the leverage of prosperity. I want to prove to you how God the creator is being treated by his own image that he created, and to analyse the implication of such an action.

Why does his existence become important here? If you believe he exists, then his intervention becomes the leverage for your encounter. Many scientists offer scientific arguments against the existence of God, and they ask this questions in favour of their conscience: Where does God play an important role in the universe? They assume that God has specific attributes that should provide objective evidence for his existence.

1. Look for such evidence with an open mind.
2. If such evidence is found, conclude that God may exist.

3. If such objective evidence is not found, conclude beyond all reasonable doubt that a God with these properties does not exist.

If these questions are directed against the creator by scholars who have fragmented knowledge as their belief, and if God still forgives us, sees to our protection, and gives us breath, then God is to be worshiped and praised because it is beyond my ability to predict the consequences if God is human just like you and me.

I am not surprised at the fugitive thoughts of humans, because Satan speaks in human form to destroy the attention of worshipping God. Satan in human form came to steal, destroy, and kill, but I can assure you that if you encounter the power of God, then Satan's mission will be returned back into misery. This is how most scientists prove that God does not exit, and it is basically how science would disprove the existence of any alleged entity, which is modified from the argument of a lack of evidence: God, as defined, should produce evidence of some sort; if we fail to find that evidence, then God cannot exist. The modification limits the sort of evidence to what can be predicted and tested. Now you see how powerful Satan is in his efforts to convince you into his kingdom.

I want you to get this straight so that you will believe in the spirit world, do away with ignorance, and run for your salvation and your encounter with God. Nothing in science is proven or disproven beyond a shadow of doubt – in science, everything is provisional. Being provisional is not a weakness or a sign that a conclusion is weak. Being provisional is a smart, pragmatic tactic because we can never be sure what we'll come across when we go around the next corner. This lack of absolute certainty is a window through which many religious theists try to slip their God, but that is not a valid move.

Again, science is all about research given out of the obscurity of nature. It is important to live life with a great encounter in order to be able to see your vision, because day-to-day activities spin the world and skip visions. The world will not favour you if you have no Christ, and it takes his encounter to see your breakthrough. In theory it may be possible that someday we will come across new information requiring or benefiting from some sort of God hypothesis in order to better make sense of the way things are. If the evidence described in the above argument was found, that would justify a rational belief in the existence of the sort of God under consideration. It wouldn't prove the existence of such a God beyond all doubt, though, because belief would still have to be provisional. By the same token, it may be possible that the same could be true of an infinite number of other hypothetical beings, forces, or things which we might invent. The mere possibility of existing is one that applies to any and every possible God, but religious theists only try to use it for whatever God they happen to personally favour.

The possibility for needing a god hypothesis applies equally as well to Zeus and Odin as it does to the Christian god; it also applies to evil or disinterested gods. Thus, even if we limit our consideration to the possibility of a god, ignoring every other random hypothesis, there's still no good reason to pick out any one god for favourable consideration. What does it mean to exist? What would it mean if "God exists" was a meaningful proposition? For such a proposition to mean anything at all, it would have to entail that whatever God is, it must have some impact on the universe. In order for us to say that there is an impact on the universe, there must be measurable and testable events that would be explained by whatever this God is. Believers must be able to present a model of the universe in which some god is either required, productive, or useful.

This is obviously not the case. Many believers work hard trying to find a way to introduce their God into scientific explanations, but none have succeeded. No believer has been able to demonstrate or even strongly suggest that there are some events in the universe which require some alleged god to explain. Instead, these constantly failing attempts end up reinforcing the impression that there are no gods and no role for them to play, and that here is no reason to give them a second thought. It is technically true that constant failures don't mean that no one will ever succeed, but it's even truer that in every other situation where failures are so consistent, we don't acknowledge any reasonable, rational, or serious reason to bother believing.

God created the heavens, the earth, and all things in them. This proclaims power, and we need power to overrule. Ruling simplifies dominion of authority to solve problems, not to create problems, so in order to merge for our act of living, we need to come across the power of the creator, who is the almighty God.

The man Isaac encountered God's power, and he was divinely favoured. From that moment his life and that of his children never remained the same. Isaac's encounter with the almighty made him one of the greatest men who ever lived (Gen. 26: 1–6). He lived at the time of famine, and things were very hard. The economy was chaotic, and all the inhabitants of the nation went through difficult times.

Isaac decided to go to Gerar, but this was not possible; Isaac then decided to go to Egypt when God told him not to go. God said, "Stay where you are, and I will be with you." Changing your environment as a solution to your problem might make your situation worse. Your only way of changing your problem location or environment is to encounter with the power of God. It is simple but powerful, and it is the finest resolution.

A young man of twenty-eight years who chose drugs to be his life killed his own mother. He was arrested and sent to jail. While in jail he killed three people within two minutes. You can see why the government changed his location, to save the others, but it was rather to the risk of others. If this boy was seen to be possessed by more than just the influence of drugs, other lives would have been saved. God is telling you right now that changing your location is not the solution, but seeking for his ways is the solution. Applying the good ways towards your future will determine your encounter.

If in the Bible we had victims of such culprits, and their solution was to encounter the power of God, then why do we litigate instead of following the simpler process? This tells you that from ancient times many have been released from bondage through encountering the power of God. Don't think you are the first and last to have problems in life. Today as you read this book, I stand by the power of God, and I command your alternative resolution to be closer to the encounter the power of God.

Why You Need to Encounter the Power of God

1. Spiritual Breakthrough

I have already enlightened you about curse inheritance from generation to generation, and it is your responsibility to know and understand the concept and how to solve it. You have a family, and so you have a curse inheritance. Spiritually, you can be blessed or cursed, but it takes the encounter to purify your destiny. If God has power over all things, then he has the power to take you away from any covenant. You need the encountering power of God for your spiritual breakthrough.

The spiritual breakthrough changes your story, and you heart will be at peace. In places where you were denied previously, you will be called because your encounter has no competitor, and your time of victory cannot be impeached by any surprise on the earth.

2. Divine Direction

The encounter gives you the mandate to your destination of victory. Therefore, you need the encounter to be well guided in all your plans, in your life or your ministry. Great men of God have their history of progression by the divine direction from God, and it takes the encounter to be able to be directed accordingly.

3. Supernatural Release

It gets you to where you didn't expect, meaning it reshapes your vision

4. Domination of Anointing

The encounter will scare your enemies because you will be anointed for a spiritual movement, and no weapon shall stop you (Zech. 4: 6).

5. Victory Outreach

Your victory will be externally known, and it shall serve as a testimony to embark on the encounter and to explore.

Chapter 7

Process to Encounter the Power of God

The principles of life give the assurance of a destination, either positive or negative, and it congregates the approval of your assignment through a required process. The meaning of this context simplifies the value of a process approved as a required procedure for conducting an exercise or a test, which has the attributes of result expectations. Under normal circumstances, every task which has result expectations attribute significant presumption for positive results, not negative; therefore along the line of the assignment, a critical appraisal of materials are substituted, and policies to govern its sector of safety are implemented. These guide components are for the purpose of reaching a successful destination.

Failure, as an opposite to success here, is seen as a forbidden trend, but no matter the description given to it, if your process does not meet your procedure, then failure becomes the result, and you will be victimized and accused because your employers will not consider the process used along the line. You are seen as the ruler of the conduct and the owner of the results, and that is the justification, not a perception.

In comparing this to reality of life, we take responsibility for whatever we do, and therefore lives at stake are determined by the prescribed procedure of living, which is considered as the required process. Looking around the world of today, the process of inventions and convections are the causes of our problems because the required process of doing things does not meet the natural, prescribed procedure to function for freedom and redemption. This is happening to personal lives, ministries, firms, organisations, institutions, and governments. I ask these questions not to purify a constructive definition of process but to clarify the norms and ethics of valuation given to a required process.

If God Almighty did not exempt a process of creation, how come we serving him devalue the required process of living? It is then important to know much about how Adam and Eve appeared on earth, and what rules were given to them as the structure to keep them preserved. You will then know that we are responsible for our own problems.

- Under what circumstances or conditions does implementation of a process qualify to guide a given task?
- How many people consider a task as a vision that will lead them to see the required process and to have the vision in hand?

If these questions are unanswered by logistics but are the accepting reality of valuation and its required process, then that forms part of the life pride enrolment of a renounced vision destiny. God in his kingdom has set up a role that separates man from bad deeds and gives man the caution of defeating his reincarnated covenants and inherited curses. The role is a simple process that one needs to sustain as a living guide to one's destiny. From the perception of world scholars, there has been a deviated definition of a process of living; that is why people are suffering, and from their configuration analysis, they consider a lack of education to be a key factor controlling such problems. This factor is conceited in a way of ignoring the acceptance of the natural basis of creation, and also covering the truth in the spiritual dominant guide process of life from the Word of God, which is the light, the truth, and the life. This automatically makes you a conqueror and a vessel.

Regarding the spiritual process mounted by God, who created heaven and earth as the main objective guide of both the spiritual and physical life, man has the strength to overcome fiscal challengers, because the knowledge of God is above all doctrines and contains all the natural, existing avenues of living. That is why academic books cannot be compared to the scripture: the scripture is not a syllable on which to conduct a test. God gives mandate to experience his glory through a process, and this process openly does not predict the mind of mankind or persuade them, but rather renders salvation into lives of men. This process has nothing to do with a prescribed education qualification or a factual principle detectable by humans – and most important, it does not reject sinners and unbelievers. It brings all to a structure of salvation. It is naturally considered to be the spiritual intervention scheme for separating you from the kingdom of darkness.

These divine processes are recognized under records of religious moral zeal, and its practice and affiliations do not deprive the pleasure of innocent people or create problems for others. It is sad that sometimes one prescribed process in life deprives the pleasure of others and creates inconveniences to friends, family, and neighbours. If this happens or is happening in your errands, then it is not a process of surviving. Your destination is not considered to be in freedom but is a curse and sorrow. Before a work of your intelligence will cross national boundaries, it must pass through a strong, systematic, required process; the process adopted holds the integral part of its function, which must be treated with care.

In spiritual confrontation, there are so many confinements in the belief of our gods, which is described as consultation. This happens for the functioning to meet the expectation of the gods to perform on our behalf. It is believed that the process of going about this consultation is the key of our gods responding to the request and fulfilling their spiritual responsibilities. Many failed to seek the right process, and so they receive nothing after the consultation is done because there was no required spiritual process of consulting the gods. The wrong way of consulting the gods sometimes can cause a hazard, which might serve as detriment to lives and entrenches the lineage of the servant.

Spiritually, through its process a covenant can be pronounced to function, and at the same time a process can be engaged for a covenant to be terminated or broken. In this case, a process is a strong activism that invokes power to wait for results.

Moses was sent by God irrespective of where he was coming from, and he was seen as a hoplite who could undertake heavy infantry. First he was surprised at who he was, to be able to carry such an assignment. It is the same thing we ask ourselves when an unexpected calling comes our way, and we get confused and react wrongly, forgetting that every being has a destiny controlled by God. Moses's conduct was a process laid down by God. It was a challenge for Moses to undertake the task because he could not speak well and had no power to control, but God said to him, "I have sent you, and by my power you will do more than what they will do. They will believe you and release my people."

Life is a journey which demands a required process to succeed. It doesn't open anywhere in the world where life seems to be straight; even if you inherit wealth, do search for the source. You will then come to realize that it was hard work which has yielded to refine your joy today, and you must also protect your children to inherit it; that is reincarnation. It is then a process that is vital to be conversant with in order to sustain what you inherit.

God gave Moses the Ten Commandments to bring God's children into the promised land. The commandments functioned under the power of God, giving authority to the hands of Moses to control the Israelites throughout the journey. This was a divine process which carried on a directive of guiding a large number of people to be under control, to regard the power of God, and to exempt them from bending out of their vision. The main objective of giving the commandments was to throw light into the view of the Israelites so that they may understand the vision of the journey. If one impeaches the fact that life is considered as a journey, then one is absolutely lost and out of success's enrolment, because it is natural fact.

Your problems are part of life; it gives you strength to be able to retreat when you are blessed, and that is why we have solutions to problems no matter the source of influence backing the situation. It has a required process to solve it, though the concept might turn to you as the most complicated and difficult zeal to handle, so that you feel the only thing to do is to kill yourself. It is a devilish thought that has consumed many on the line of their problems, but today I challenge you to defeat it. It is a supplication that consumes fire; the process to undertake and to receive is simplistic activism. It is not a process to get someone executed, or a process to tarnish and deprive the pleasure of innocent souls.

God has given us the power to control and to rebuke, but it takes a process to be able to enforce the command to take effect, because it determines how you regard the process and obey it. The one who obeys God's commandments has automatically taken the process of experiencing the power of the encounter. It sanctifies your spirit and gives you anointing to be regarded and favoured, and your story changes from bad to good. A great respect and attention is given to the federal house and other superior halls in the states because their process and functions do not condone disobedience. Therefore maximum attention and respect must be given to the supernatural being who created heaven and earth. How many times have you succeeded when a work was done without identifying the required process, and how did it treat you with its returns? This is happening in businesses, ministries, and affairs; things are done without identifying a required process to meet its success. Your required process determines how you want your ministry to grow. I am happy that God spoke to me years back, and by the practice of obedience all has come to pass because whatever God has pronounced, no man can terminate it – but it takes the heart of an obedient child to receive the blessing in the form of encountering the power of God.

God spoke to me in a dream. I was walking with my spiritual father towards a narrow road, and in the dream I could see that it was a long journey because in response to the distance, my breath was choked, which describes total tiredness. It seemed I was being pulled back by an unseen spirit, but my spiritual father was relaxed and kept moving. He turned back and asked me if I was tired. I didn't understand the question because he knew I was tired. He said to me, "Until you wear this white cloth, you can never get to the destination." He helped me change the cloth to the one he gave me, and a few minutes after I put on the new cloth, something entered me and I started walking comfortably. Before we got to where we were going, he gave me a rod and said, "By this rod you can clear this bush." I walked up and had a flashback to five years ago and dream I'd had when I was struggling on the ground and trying to take a rod. I was surprised that God showed me the meaning of the rod: through his process I could move the rod to clear the bush. Now my ministry in Hamburg is clearing the bush with the given rod from God; miracles are taking place not by the shouting and proclaiming but by the Word of God.

Encountering the power of God affects lives when a process is undertaken in spirit, seeking a breakthrough. A process for encountering the power of God is not static in nature or peculiar; it is very dynamic and has no special environment to influence its effect. That is why God is omnipotent: he sees all things and takes advice from no man before sharing his grace. Now you can understand the reality of God's power, which is ready to deal with your problems drastically if you accept him as your God and personal saviour. You consider yourself a sinner with no value. You think your life is complicated because of accusations from people, you seem dejected that every environment does not accept you, and you experience signs of unexpected problems. I can promise you that today marks the critical juncture of your endeavour and is the beginning of your transformation.

Whenever there is a process, and results are analysed and remarks are given to the process, it doesn't matter whether or not it was through a required process. What matters is the result, which defines the process that was engaged, because the outcome is either positive or negative. In comparing this to spiritual world, through a process the covenant can function effectively, and at the same time a process can be engaged for a covenant to be terminated. Process is a strong setup that invokes power to wait for the results.

Encountering the power of God avails upon lives; when a process is undertaken in spirit, it feeds the soul to resort by the word, which is the truth and the light of the world. A process of encountering the power of God is not static in nature but is very dynamic. It defines the miraculous ways in which God works. Sometimes you can see a problem getting closer, and you will do your best to prevent it, but you get betrayed by what you try to prevent. You then curse your own mistakes and call it a defeat to your soul. However, later you realise that problem happened for a reason. God's ways are beyond understanding.

There are so many ways God visits you to experience his grace, but in all of them there is a process you envision for the grace, considering yourself as a sinner with no value before God. This definition wrongly predicts that the minds of victims will not come to Christ because it is the fusion of the devil to deceive unbelievers. Today I don't predict the mind of you, and neither am I persuading you. God loves sinners, and he protects them and gives them shelter, food, and clothes. Thousands of angels in heaven rejoice and see to the sinners' encounters as soon as they repent and give their lives to Christ. God always wants to prove the difference between the world and his kingdom, and he uses the voyages of sinners to counter the laments of unbelievers.

God's power rules in the lives of mankind, and there are so many ways we use it to proclaim and make it function. If God has laid down his ways of giving us freedom, then it is our choice to get hold of the process to experience it. The process of encountering the power of God is described in two ways: through a special engagement process of encountering the power of God (request), and through an automatic explosion of the encounter (favour).

Through a Special Engagement Process for the Encounter (Request)

This is the fruit you enjoy after you have planted the seed on fertile soil. Your expectation to enjoy the fruit of your labour becomes a priority, and your days and seasons during the harvest period are your success. Considering the factors of sowing the seed are the subsequently required in the process of good futures for harvest. This is compared to how we accept the chapter of the word that requires a process of encountering the power of God. The Word of God gives us a vibrant process of becoming a vessel and a testimony to others, and through that process your encounter comes into reality. This is a determining factor that puts you in charge of making a relevant emotional request from God, and it serves as a trademark of becoming born again. Spiritually it is considered as the first step of encountering the power of God. The Bible said obedience is better than sacrifice; it simplifies an attention deserved in the episode of worshiping God in faith and honesty, because to worship Jesus is a process you must know, understand, practice, and share in order to avail the purpose of creation.

The special engagement process starts when you cordially comply with the divine spiritual process. It is a request you engage with faith, honesty, commitment, and submission. Spiritually, God intervenes and acts according to a process you laid in order to embark on a request. This can be done when you understand spiritual enforcement, because anything that happens in the physical has already happened in the spiritual; that is why God has spread gifts of many kinds to his servants, and why he is able to see and invoke against it through a divinely given process. Encountering the power of God is a spiritual movement that takes control over destiny regardless of your spiritual background, so the process to acquire the encounter under this phenomenon is a request and vigorously seeks for his power to intervene.

The Special Process Engaged for the Request

Step 1: Repentance

Repentance is your heart accepting Jesus Christ as your personal saviour and believing in his resurrection after he suffered on the cross. Jesus Christ was on earth for a purpose: to save mankind from the misery caused by sins. This defines salvation because according to the scripture, sin is the great obstacle of man having a strong relationship with the father who lives in heaven. Repentance therefore becomes a great redemption for mankind because it is the exchange of the blood of the son for our sins, committed by our ignorance and persecutions. That is why God is a merciful God to his people and forgives our sins. If one repents, it gives him the mandate of spiritual comprehensive understanding to the Word of God, and he automatically gains spiritual strength, which assists in his rising from the kingdom of darkness. He is entitled to receive God's grace upon his life. The moment a sinner regrets his or her doings, the devil becomes weak and frustrated because the mind has been purified by the Holy Spirit. The activism of the victim begins to change, and he is spiritually moved to search for resolution. In the spiritual realm, the soul begins to seek spiritual food, which is the Word of God. Repentance becomes the first step for God to come into your life, because Jesus Christ has already paid for your sins. Your resolution is not by your strength but the truth of the word, which qualifies you to have your instant salvation. Repentance stands as your first step to be accepted into his grace as a child of God, and so it is part of the process to encounter the power of God because your salvation is the first encounter.

Step 2: Effectiveness in Word

In our Christian lives, many have deviated and have come short of the glory of God because there are many perspectives of the definition of Christianity, according to believers. This deviation has led to a practice that fails to function under the norms and ethics of the Word of God. Therefore many live under the same roof and the same environment with others with great testimonies; this means they undermine the concept of Christianity. If Christianity is seen to be the way of Christ followed by mankind, then you will have your means to serve God. The Word of God is the strength and the weapon of every Christian; it contains the power to overcome all avenues of demonic operations, and it sustains your life under God's protection. You need to be active in the word, and it qualifies your stage to meet the power of God in your life.

Step 3: Commitment

Commitment stands in at your release when good and perfect attention is given to it, and it forms part of all the components subjected to your encounter. The level of expectation in everyday activities are recorded and analysed, and a lot of life's choices are considered, but commitment carries the day because commitment is accelerated in serving God and is a leverage of compliance with the definition of the word. The Word of God is to share with us the truth, salvation, and worship – but without commitment, it is likely we will lack the influence of the word. As I have already said, worshiping God from the heart is the definition of the purpose of creation, because God created humans for the reason of his existence, and the response to this existence is done by worshiping and praising him. Even though many don't understand the meaning of worship, share with them a testimony out of worship; it automatically proves the merits of commitments.

Jesus Christ was committed to his assignment. He was ready for the battle, and salvation for the children of God was the subject of his assignment. He knew the benefits to mankind if he succeeded. It is therefore our assignment to be committed in accepting Jesus Christ as our personal saviour, and we must believe, worship, and exhort him as the son of God. Commitment, with the significance of serving God from the heart, is considered to be part of your process to make a request from God. It is a conduct of preserving yourself to experience an encounter with the power of God. Commitment does not deal with just one area in life: Determination in your career is about commitment, making your ministry a recognised one across boundaries requires the work of commitment, and expectation of your request from God is your commitment. Now you see how good and soundly living demands commitment. If you understand the route of making justifications for success, then it is up to you to address your start and be full of commitment.

All these affiliations of submitting to a particular task or worship add up as a process of reaching one's destiny, which is success. Commitment becomes a component of encountering the power of God because it is the domain in which God sees and rewards. He hears and responds to requests, and he is at the door, so whoever listens and open, he will come and stay in the heart.

Do not fret because of the evil men or be envious of those who do wrong for like the grass they will soon

> wither, like green plant, they will soon die. Trust in
> the lord and do good. Dwell in the land and enjoy
> safe pasture. Delight yourself in the lord and he will
> give you the desire of your heart Commit your ways
> to the lord, trust in him and he will do this He will
> make your righteousness shine like the dawn. The
> justice of your cause like noonday sun. (Ps. 37: 1–11)

Though the devil is always at work trying to frustrate us, and temptations are taking seats to get us separated from God, you should commit your ways into the hands of the Lord. That is where you encounter the power of God, and He will make your righteousness shine like the dawn. The dawn here symbolises life or mood without interference.

Automatic Explosion of the Encounter (Divine Favour)

This is the encounter that deals with the supernatural release to intervene unexpectedly. It takes effect on a platform to catalyze revenge on your enemies in a way of natural explosion. This encounter invokes extraordinary power to cut the trend of the evil errands from Satan. The automatic explosion of the encounter is a divine favour that takes place under the roof of worship and praises. God created man in his own image, and the purpose of creating man is to get the grace of worship from man; that is why the power of God is explored, and many encounter the power of God automatically when worship is emotionally conducted with faith.

I understand the strength of the masses thinking of Christianity as a religion, but today I declare that if

Christianity will mean to you not just a religion but a style of worship, then you will see and receive the automatic explosion of the encounter. Jesus said, "If you don't praise me, I will command the stones to rise up and praise me." Automatic explosion of the encounter accelerates in times of difficulties, when dreams have been washed away, priorities are deformed, accusations have tarnished image to shame, sensational news has wiped away hope. You may feel the only thing left is to kill yourself, but God intervenes when you set yourself to put a practice of attention to him, and I can assure you that God is faithful in intervening in your situation, no matter who you are or how you see yourself. Simply enter in worship, forget about the pain, and thank him for the problem. I know this will be hard for some: "How can I enter into thanksgiving when God has not solved a problem for me?" You wonder how it is possible for your emotions to sustain the treasure of pains and to enter into worship while you can see your problem bleeding. This is the weapon against your enemies, and it is a leverage of experiencing the automatic explosion of the encounter.

In the spiritual realm, the sensitivity of your soul attracts joy, and your heart corresponds with comfort when your enemies are defeated. I strongly believe that this chapter of the book can be a challenge to your faith, but it will also be the chapter of your testimony. It will serve as your weapon to understand how God works in mysterious ways, through worship and praise.

The Norms and Ethics of Worship and Praises That Explore the Power Encounter

How can this automatic power explosion for an encounter take effect, and under what state or condition does one meet the explosion acceleration? This indicates that God does not confine anyone before speaking into our lives, and for him to intervene in our problems, there is a need to undertake divine steps that have something to do with the heart, body, and soul. The heart demands a cordial relation with belief and faith; this generates redemptive measures to the soul. The environment witnessing your existence will be determined by the body, because the image will describe the vision and the reality of God's power. God said that he created man in his own image, and he referred to the body as his church; whoever destroys the body, so he will destroy him. He created you and had plans to protect what he created.

Whenever failure or disappointment comes our way, the soul gets defeated, but failure does not mean the end of life. These are life trends that form part of reality, and accepting that gives you the determination to move on because it is a sign of your acceptance of reality. It is then considered to be an experience to move you on. God said that man will suffer before attaining his consumption, and a woman will feel the pain before giving birth; this throws so many challenges into our lives, but he said that he has the power to intervene in our situations. If sorrow becomes your reaction, then it is obvious that you have lost the battle. Sorrow then causes a trench in your mind and leads you to defeat. God is merciful: he comes into situations that cause bitterness before they generate rigidity in life. Bitterness that generates rigidity has frustrated and killed a lot of people, but it is a viable contempt against the human right and against creation, and so God intervenes with the highest favour to rescue victims and reform their lives.

God becomes the first step in the process of automatic explosion. If you get rid of sorrow when you are in the presence of God during a form of worship, it means you have valued the power of God. This connects to faith, and God at the moment rescues you. From the moment you start to worship, try to take off your problems from your mind and stay focused on his existence. May you have a testimony when you engage in this first step as a process of experiencing the automatic power explosion of God.

During Worship

Strong Worship Dialogue

Worshiping God is the communication you have with him, telling him what he has done through a passionate and emotional delivery and using sensitive dialogue, uplifting his grace upon your life. This communication invokes God's power automatically. If worship is engaged deeply from the heart, then angels descend and uplift your desires to God. There are so many constructions of dialogues to put the heart into spirit, and the diversities of the dialogues have their destinations, but one's ability to praise and give thanks connects directly to the purpose of his creation. This service is admired by the heavens and resends grace to function upon you, which causes a lot of powerful integration in the spiritual realm to change lives.

Functions of Strong Worship Dialogues

1. Strong worship dialogues break covenants because it throws challenge to God, and he acts immediately.
2. Strong worship dialogues intervene against hidden trenches and break them down.
3. Strong worship dialogues feed the soul with joy, especially when engaging in songs of praise.
4. Strong worship dialogues determine your faith in the service of his word.
5. Strong worship dialogues serve as a weapon to destroy the works of the enemy.
6. Strong worship dialogues are the keys to experience testimony in your life.

During Praises

Activism Engaged on Praises

Praises is the core activity under the automatic explosion of encountering the power of God. It contains norms of powerful messages and activities that please God. The message is conducted in the form of music, and the activity is conducted in a form of dancing. These two areas combine together to experience the explosion of the power of God.

When God is being praised, miracles take place and people are healed from their sickness. When the heart is purified and is eager to praise his name, that is where joy takes place, ignoring all kinds of problems; favour takes control. Favour can be in the form of miracles, financial breakthrough, fruitfulness, and many other good things in life.

Praise comes in a form of music which contains a message of praising God, and when the message is filled with anointing, dancing takes place, and miracles happen.

Functions of Praise

1. Praises take off stress through music and dancing. They plant joy and hope in the heart and into the lives of people.
2. Through praises, your enemies will be silent because when God is praised, enemies cannot operate.
3. Praises destroy the work of the enemies (Ps. 8: 2).
4. Praises change the environment.
5. Praises employ the anointing and get the Holy Spirit to work

Chapter 8

Sealing the Encounter

Whatever you have secured and acquired in life throughout your long journey seems to be very important to you. It is nature, and nature is said to be the origin of everything. Such accomplishment was seen to be a strong vision you had, and gradually on your mission you adequately got to that target. You have no option than to develop the heart's desire to protect it. The mandate of your destination to your vision reminds you always about how you struggled on the road toward the vision, with both obstacles and opportunities you met on the way, but the memories of the obstacles are the major highlight here. They enhance your strength to protect what you acquired, because it's your success, and you cannot jeopardize it in any way.

Sometimes I wonder how one jeopardises his relationship with his master who gave him all things he needed in life. God is the supernatural controller of all things; his kingdom accepts those who value and keep his covenant, because if you value your covenant with God, it automatically seals your covenant with him. The reality of valuation determines your implementation towards your heart's desire, and therefore your valuation towards the encounter will determine your actions to seal your encounter. The only strong spiritual element to seal the encounter is your fiduciary covenant with God.

Fiduciary covenant is the role and the responsibilities you undertake to keep your encounter functioning effectively. This avails the Holy Spirit to work under the control of God's authority, and nothing can be compared to your life because your soul will have external life. Many people with great visions have had the encounter, and heaven has opened for the glory to descend upon them. Captivities have come to an end, lamentation has ceased to function, great clouds have raged with fire, and enemies have been executed. This defines the encounter, yet they failed to protect the encounter because they lose the trend of their covenant with God. I want you to understand that if you fail God, God don't retaliate, but it is the covenant's retribution that gets you punished. Do not value your acquired property more than the covenant, because the property you have now cannot sustain the covenant. It is rather the covenant that sustains what you have through your encounter of God.

I panic and get scared when I see one who values home materials more than the Word of God, because the consequences are beyond my ability to predict. Today I stand as a man of God, and I curse every demon that enforces your activism to devalue the word in Jesus's name. Encountering the power of God lifts you to your vision in life, and jeopardising your relationship with God in order to keep what you have acquired is the last mistake you will make in life. Implementing spiritual components of the covenant to seal your encounter will help you enjoy everlasting success.

Hence forth, I want you to understand that in spiritual world, encountering the power of God demands the spiritual protection to seal the encounter which is fiduciary covenant with God to retain the growth of the Holy Spirit in you to be able to enjoy your refines forever.

Major Factors to Seal Your Acquired Encounter

1. Spiritual Fiduciary Covenant (Having a Responsible Covenant with God)

A spiritual fiduciary is a vital and valuable role that takes on many responsibilities of good faith and moral judgement in spiritual matters, as well as accessing a process of attention to be able to make an impact on your valuable acquisitions in life. Encountering the power of God automatically lights up your opportunities and takes absolute control over your life in successful ways. Therefore, your role both physically and spiritually must be a fiduciary covenant to seal your encounter. In the reality of life, if you know your role, you don't deviate and never bend out of enrolment. As such you will understand your duties, and credibility will come your way; your work will cross national boundaries, and you will be recognized.

Covenants demand a role from partners regardless of who formed it or receives it. One needs to play one's part to keep the covenant. God is a covenant-keeping God who never fails, and when you attend to your responsibility, then you are an overcomer, and nothing can stop you from reaching the sky. A covenant with God is a great spiritual duty of good faith, trust, confidence, sacrifice, and holiness in God. This spiritual component of the covenant seals the encounter because it closes every hole Satan could use to shut down the encounter. These spiritual components feed your spirit with a strong perseverance for the Holy Spirit to work actively in your life, which defines the seal of your encounter.

2. Holiness in Serving God

Holiness has escaped the attention that it deserves in both of our physical, spiritual, private, and public lives, and the strength of its implication is deadly. I ask you these questions.

- In your physical life, how do you relate to others? Does your life cause detriment to others' welfare, or deprive the pleasure of innocent people?
- In your spiritual life, how are you faithful to God?
- In your private life, where do you find yourself, and how does the environment affect your private life?
- In your public life, do you play a role to set good records and to bring people to Christ, or do you serve as an agent of the devil?

When holiness becomes a fiduciary covenant with God, peace and salvation will be your portion. When the Passover of the Jews was at hand, Jesus went up to Jerusalem. The Bible says he found in the temple those who sold oxen and sheep and doves, and the money changers doing business. When he made a whip of cord, he drove them all out of the temple with the sheep and the oxen, and he poured out the changers and overturned the tables. He said to them all, "Take these things away, do not make my father's house a house of merchandise."

This was a sign, action and words proving to the Jews the norms and ethics of the temple, which is holiness, so that it may be holy forever. This means in the Bible the only practise that caused Jesus to be angry was when holiness was abused. Jesus said again to them, "If you destroy this temple, in three days I will raise it up." They were confused because it took them forty-six years to build the temple, but Jesus was speaking of the temple of his body, and without holiness there would be no faith for Jesus to talk about resurrection. Holiness must be preserved and manifested by your body and soul, as a covenant with God to control your life. This meets the expectation of the encounter and seals itself to open heaven for your everlasting breakthrough. Holiness is a covenant-sealed component that is relevant before, during, and after encountering the power of God.

Holiness before the encounter is a core preparation to the encounter. During the encounter holiness makes restoration take place, and after the encounter holiness seals the success. Therefore holiness is a covenant component that demands your compliance to get it moved, and if your spiritual fiduciary to God does not operate under the cord of holiness, then you cease the anointing and pause the work of the Holy Spirit; you will receive nothing because you devalue the encounter, and he will not pay its pride fiduciary in your life.

3. Wisdom of God

Wisdom of God fulfils the responsibility of sealing your encounter with God, and it entrenches your restoration in so many divine diversities. In the reality of life, I have come to believe that opportunities come across our path and are recognized by the wisdom placed in our repository by the creator, but due to acquisition of knowledge through education, we ignore the evidence of the natural wisdom of God's fulfilment. The critical and logical thinking that subscribe to professional delivery cannot work if God does not approve by giving you his wisdom to apply, irrespective of your academic background. God's wisdom holds the power to control and to overcome.

> A man of knowledge who increases in strength and by wisdom you will wage your own war and in multitude of counsellors there is safety, said the lord. (Prov. 24: 5)

The passage means that in both the physical and spiritual life, we need wisdom because without wisdom, knowledge cannot be recognised. Indeed, God is a faithful God, and wisdom is greater than knowledge (Prov. 24: 3–4). Through wisdom a house is built, and through understanding it is established. With knowledge the rooms are filled with all precious and pleasant riches. I want you to study this chart, which differentiates the application of knowledge without wisdom and that of knowledge and wisdom.

Chart 1

Wants before Needs Chart (Knowledge without Wisdom)

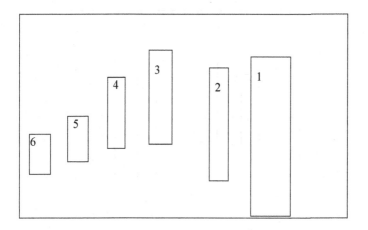

This system takes you from behind downwards and it ends you in extra cost

This is when you have a list of what you are to buy for the week consumption at the market. You first had the knowledge to write a list but didn't apply wisdom to list it in scale of adequate preference therefore you bought things you want before buying what you need. When you start the usage, you realise the wants will demand the needs and that leads to extra cost from your account. Debt will be around you and you will go bankrupt. You created problem for yourself because of lack of wisdom.

Chart 2

Needs before Wants (Knowledge and Wisdom)

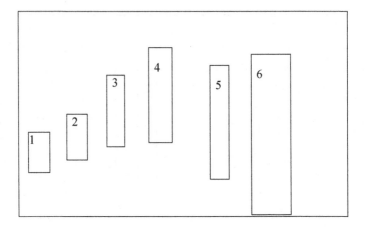

This is the system that runs normally from top down, which defines normal and the correct system of managing without extra cost. This is when you have the knowledge to write a list of what you have to buy, and you apply wisdom to make it on the scale of presence in order to get rid of the extra cost for wants.

Today, do not be scared about the concept of your problems; it might be your mistakes that have caused you to be hated by people, but it can also be a lack of experience that has created complications. Maybe your personal friend is responsible for pressing charges against you, putting you to trial and condemning you to death. Do not be afraid because through the encounter your story is going to change, and the wisdom of God will take place to seal the encounter.

How Does Wisdom Seal the Encounter?

Wisdom is simply a role to play in order to seal the encounter. It is a core responsibility that needs to be given attention regardless of the structure of your covenant with God. Spiritually, it affirms the everlasting glory of God to shine upon your life.

Your Role to Play under Wisdom to Protect the Encounter

Pray for wisdom to sow seeds in the house of God to get your covenant at work.

Pray for wisdom to pay your tithe for financial breakthrough.

Pray for wisdom to end your battle with enemies.

Pray for wisdom to keep secrets of your vision and to allow the Holy Spirit to take absolute control.

Finally, pray for wisdom to keep your access to the house of God.